PANZERS FORWARD

PANZERS FORWARD

A Photo History of
German Armor in World War II

Robert J. Edwards

With Contributions by
Michael Olive and Michael H. Pruett

STACKPOLE
BOOKS

x

GUILFORD, CT

STACKPOLE
BOOKS

Published by Stackpole Books
An imprint of The Rowman & Littlefield Publishing Group, Inc.
4501 Forbes Blvd., Ste. 200
Lanham, MD 20706
www.rowman.com

Distributed by NATIONAL BOOK NETWORK
800-462-6420

British Library Cataloguing in Publication Information available

Library of Congress Cataloging-in-Publication Data available

ISBN 978-0-8117-3770-8 (paperback)
ISBN 978-0-8117-6742-2 (e-book)

∞™ The paper used in this publication meets the minimum requirements of
American National Standard for Information Sciences—Permanence of Paper for
Printed Library Materials, ANSI/NISO Z39.48-1992.

Printed in the United States of America

Contents

SS-Kriegsberichter Böhm's sketch interpretation of the recovery version of the *Panther* tank, the *Bergepanther*, recovering a disabled *Panther* on the Eastern Front. About 400 *Bergepanthers* were produced or converted from 1943 to 1945. Böhm served with *SS-Standarte "Kurt Eggers,"* which was the front-line propaganda element of the *SS* Headquarters (*SS-Hauptamt*). This illustration was prepared for press release on November 30, 1944. (MICHAEL H. PRUETT)

FACING PAGE TOP: This photograph, possibly taken at a training establishment during the last years of the war, shows an early *Panzer V, Ausführung D "Panther."* The vehicle has a coating of *Zimmerit*—a concrete-like substance applied to exposed surfaces of armored vehicles to defeat antimagnetic mines used by the Soviet Union—and a single-digit white numeral *8* appears on the side of the turret. Based on the *Zimmerit* pattern, the tank was probably manufactured by Daimler-Benz or *Maschinenfabrik Niedersachsen Hannover (MNH)*. Of particular interest is the *Panzer IV* in the background. This vehicle appears to have liquid propane gas bottles affixed to its rear as an alternate source of fuel. Only a handful of *Panzer IV*s were converted to use this method of providing vehicular power, and they were only used in the training base because of the high volatility and vulnerability of the fuel. Other photographs seen by the authors show the bottles mounted vertically as well. (MICHAEL H. PRUETT)

FACING PAGE BOTTOM: Taken at a training installation, possibly for a *Panzerjäger-Ersatz und Ausbildungs-Abteilung* (antitank replacement and training detachment), this photograph shows five noncommissioned officers (NCOs) posing in front of an *Sd.Kfz. 132 Panzer Selbstfahrlafette 1 für 7.62cm auf Fahrgestell Panzerkampfwagen II*, the first version of the self-propelled antitank gun based on the *Panzer II* chassis. The vehicle is painted in an overall coat of dark yellow (*dunkelgelb*) and featured a captured Russian 7.62cm antitank gun rechambered for German ammunition. Approximately 200 of these vehicles were produced between 1942 and 1943.

Most of the NCOs are also officer candidates—indicated by the double loops of silver braid at the base of their shoulder straps—and have seen service at the front, as evidenced by their decorations. The *Feldwebel* standing on the left wears the single-handed tank destruction badge on his right sleeve, which was introduced in March 1942 but could be awarded for actions dating back to June 1941. Two of the NCOs (second and fourth from the left) wear M-1943 pattern trousers with gaiters, further aiding in establishing a time frame for this photograph. (MICHAEL H. PRUETT)

ABOVE: The ubiquitous German assault gun, the *Sturmgeschütz III*—possibly the *Ausführung F2*, the first to be armed with the longer 75mm gun—as it appeared in a line drawing for a wartime recruiting brochure. With more than 9,000 vehicles produced in at least seven major variants and a host of minor ones, it was Germany's most manufactured assault gun. The "poor man's tank" was initially intended to provide "backbone" to infantry elements. By the end of the war, it was also being issued to tank battalions in addition to assault gun brigades.

ABOVE: GIs and a Sherman pass a knocked-out *Sturmgeschütz III* somewhere in Germany, presumably in the spring of 1945. The assault gun sports a typical three-color camouflage scheme seen starting in 1943. It featured a base coat of *dunkelgelb* (dark yellow) with stripes of *rotbraun* (red-brown) and *olivgrün* (olive green) applied over it. There were wide variations in the applications of these colors, since it was basically left up to the unit to apply them in the field, as conditions allowed. Whether the dark-splotch "hand" on the main gun recoil mechanism jacket is intentional on the part of the soldier who applied the camouflage or coincidental as a byproduct of spraying is open to conjecture. (MICHAEL H. PRUETT)

FACING PAGE BOTTOM: Designed in 1932 and entering production in 1934, the *Panzer I* saw service in the Spanish Civil War as part of the *Legion Condor*. Although considered primarily a training tank by 1939, it saw combat action into 1941, and many variants based on its chassis—including command vehicles, driver-training vehicles, self-propelled antitank guns, self-propelled infantry support vehicles, armored engineer vehicles and bridge layers, flamethrowers, antiaircraft gun carriers, and armored ammunition resupply vehicles—were used until the end of the war by the German armed forces. The *Panzer I* seen here features the prewar *Buntfarbenanstrich* (multi-color paint pattern) consisting of *erdgelb-matt* (matte earth yellow), *braun-matt* (matte brown), and *grün-matt* (matte green). This scheme was replaced in 1937 by a simpler pattern consisting of two colors, *dunkelbraun* (dark brown) and *dunkelgrau* (dark gray) on new vehicles, with the original scheme to be retained on older vehicles until the vehicle needed to be repainted. Sometimes a narrow band of black was used to separate the camouflage colors. The diminutive size of the vehicle can be seen by the tankers posed next to it. No machine guns have been mounted, which was often the case with vehicles being used for training or demonstration purposes.

A British/Commonwealth soldier poses in front of a captured/abandoned *leichte Feldhaubitze 18M* in the North African desert. The 10.5cm howitzer was the standard medium artillery piece of German divisions throughout the war and was generally fielded to two of the three battalions of the divisional artillery regiment. It had a five-man crew, a maximum range of nearly 11,000 meters, and a theoretical rate of fire of between four and six rounds a minute. Of interest is the abandoned equipment surrounding the gun and the camouflage netting draped over it. (TONY ORMANDY/JEFFREY PLOWMAN)

Introduction

German armored vehicles and weapons of the World War II period have always held a peculiar fascination for military history buffs, armored vehicle enthusiasts, and scale model builders. It is the intent of this work to provide the reader with previously unpublished photographs or those that have seldom been seen except in publications not available to the general public.

Whether the reader has followed the subject for a long time or has only recently developed an interest in the topic, we hope to appeal to both ends of the spectrum—in the first instance through offering heretofore unseen material, and in the second by providing context for what is being seen.

The wartime photographs used in this book come primarily from the following original sources:

- Official photographers: There were members of front-line propaganda companies whose job was to photograph not only combat actions but also the daily routines of the German soldier. These images are not unlike those of the US Army Signal Corps in that they were professionally photographed but also often staged. They were generally intended for home-front consumption and frequently presented a romantic view of the war effort.

- Amateur photographers: German soldiers often took their personal cameras to the front with them to record their experiences. These snapshots ranged in quality from crudely composed and over- or underexposed images to photographs of almost professional quality. Although subjected to censorship, they still often provided a less glamorous view of the war. While the subject matter frequently consisted of mundane images of comrades and routine life at the front, many images also offer a treasure trove of information for those interested in the subject: regulation and non-regulation uniform details, rare or heretofore undiscovered variants and field modifications to vehicles, or camouflage and markings that had not previously seen the light of day, to name but a few.

- Allied soldiers: Like their German adversaries, these soldiers often brought cameras from home to the front lines. In addition, high-quality cameras captured from German prisoners were treasured souvenirs and would be used by the Allied soldiers to take their own personal snapshots. American GIs seemed to take particular enjoyment in photographing captured or destroyed German vehicles, and it is due in no small part to them that we have many excellent, uncensored photographs of obscure vehicles and unit markings today.

Augmenting the period black-and-white images is a color section that features prewar and wartime images from the collection of Akira Takiguchi, which offer a number of fascinating insights into markings and camouflage.

While the images are the "stars" of this photo album, we have taken great pains to properly caption them as well as provide detailed information about the "forensic" evidence provided in the photos that allows us to make certain judgment calls as to location, date, and operational status where none have been provided to us. As always, there is room for error in such judgment calls, and we welcome such information as readers may be able to provide to update future editions of this book to make it even better.

We have provided a cursory summary of the numerous engagements, battles, and sweeping campaigns that these armored vehicles were involved in. It is intended as an overview of some of the more important theaters of war and certainly not an attempt to replace any of the hundreds of excellent books written on the topic. These summaries concentrate on the armored vehicles that were most commonly encountered in the theater in question.

Once again, hundreds if not thousands of books are available on these vehicles, many of them covering the subject in almost obsessive detail. At the end of the book, we have provided a list of titles where the uninitiated may begin their search for more information. Our focus will be to provide an outline of how these vehicles evolved in response to lessons learned on the battlefield and how new vehicles, primarily tanks and self-propelled guns, were introduced in an effort to gain combat supremacy.

As with any subject that garners such passionate devotees, there are often conflicting viewpoints on the efficacy of many of the weapons systems under discussion. We will try to remain dispassionate in our discussions, but our opinions will also color the debate from time to time.

Luftwaffe personnel man a motion-picture camera, possibly capturing images for use in a weekly newsreel. Images used in this book come from official sources and amateur front-line photographers from both sides.

Should our efforts meet with success, we hope to provide additional volumes of images in the future.

Acknowledgments and Credits

This book would not have been possible without the efforts of a number of people who generously gave of their time, knowledge, photographic assistance, and encouragement. In particular, we wish to acknowledge the invaluable assistance provided by Martin Block, Bob Burden, Barry Crook, Paul Genader, John Jay Nelson, Ken Nieman, Tony M. Ormandy, Jeff Plowman, Akira Takiguchi, Detlev Terlisten, and Martin Stiles. If we have omitted anyone, we are truly sorry for the oversight.

Robert J. Edwards
Michael H. Pruett
Michael Olive

CHAPTER 1

The Prewar German Armored Force (1935–39)

One of the many harsh dictates of the 1919 Treaty of Versailles was the reduction of the German armed forces, now called the *Reichswehr*, to a maximum of 100,000 troops, with no armored vehicles other than a few armored cars, no heavy artillery, and no aircraft. The General Staff was also to be disbanded, a provision very difficult to enforce and fairly easy for the Germans to circumvent.

The head of the *Truppenamt* (Troop Office)—essentially the General Staff—was *Generaloberst* Hans von Seeckt, an enthusiastic supporter of the concepts of operational mobility and maneuver warfare. Conceptually, a highly mobile force was necessary if the small German Army were forced to fight a war on two fronts. This was a valid proposition, considering that Germany faced potential opponents in France, Poland, and Czechoslovakia in the 1920s. This receptiveness toward mobility produced a favorable climate for the eventual creation of an armored force.

Heinz Guderian has been credited with being the "Father of the German Armored Force" and there is much justification in this assessment. Without a doubt, Guderian was one of the driving forces in the establishment of the *Panzerwaffe* (armored force). In 1922, after service primarily as a staff officer in the Great War, as it was then known, Guderian was transferred to the Inspectorate of Motorized Troops, Motorized Transport Division. Initially his appointment was on the technical side, concerned more with the mechanics of motorization—maintenance, fuel depots, and the like—and not the tactical and operational aspects of the employment of motorized forces.

In time, however, Guderian began conceptualizing a role for motorized forces that was designed to break the impasse and slaughter of trench warfare and reintroduce mobility to the

FACING PAGE: A *Panzer I* seems to be the center of attention during a celebration, as it is led by a noncommissioned officer at a walking pace down a crowded city street. The fledgling panzer forces of Germany garnered attention whenever they appeared in public, partially symbolizing the resurgence of German power after the humiliating defeat of World War I and the resented terms of the subsequent Treaty of Versailles. The white numbering on the hull is the vehicle chassis number, as provided by the manufacturer. In all, nearly 1,700 vehicles were produced as tanks, with several hundred more produced as command and control variants and nearly 500 as training vehicles. (MICHAEL H. PRUETT)

battlefield. In Germany, one influence was General von Tschischwitz, who wrote about the use of motorized vehicles in transport troops, and Guderian came to the conclusion that the protection of those forces in combat could only be accomplished with armored vehicles. Guderian also read books and articles by British armor theorists and contemporaries such as Martel, Fuller, and Hart, with the latter being a particularly strong advocate of the concentration of armor for long-range operations against enemy lines of communication and the employment of combined-arms tactics. Guderian began to combine these ideas with his own and became a forceful adherent of armored warfare through his writing in professional journals of the time, such as the *Militär-Wochenblatt* (*The Military Weekly*). His ideas and influence began to spread throughout the Army of the Weimar Republic.

Progress in this regard was also seen elsewhere in the small peacetime force. In the winter of 1923–24, *Oberstleutnant* von Brauchitsch, who later became the commander in chief of the army, organized an exercise to explore the potential of motorized troops acting in concert with supporting aircraft. In 1925 furtive technical specifications for the progenitors of armored fighting vehicles were issued. One of these was the *Großtraktor* (large tractor), which weighed 20 tons, was armed with a 75mm cannon, had a top speed of 40kph, and was manned by a crew of six. The name was intended to deceive Allied armaments inspectors.

In 1926 the farsighted General von Vollard-Bockelburg was installed as the head of the motorized troops, and the *Kraftfahrtruppen* were soon redesignated as the *Kraftfahrkampftruppen*, or motorized combat troops. That same year, the Germans and Soviets concluded an agreement allowing the Germans to hold tank trials near Kazan on the River Kama in the Soviet Union. The Soviets did not provide any tanks for the secret training facility, so training did not actually commence until the prototype *Großtraktor* arrived in 1928. Six of these were eventually actually built. They were of limited use from a tactical training perspective, but engineers, designers, and potential manufacturers learned valuable lessons that went into future German armored vehicle development.

Following a period of three years as an instructor in tactics and military history at the Army Training Department, Guderian was asked by *Oberst* Stottmeister of the Motor Transport Instructional Staff to instruct his staff in tank tactics in conjunction with transporting troops by truck. Exercises were conducted with dummy tanks—mock-ups of tanks with canvas frames mounted on trucks—much to the amusement of the infantry, who bayoneted them at every opportunity.

In 1929 Guderian experienced driving a tank for the first time, when he visited Sweden. The vehicle in question was an M29, a derivative of the *Leichter Kampfwagen II* (*LKII*), designed by Joseph Vollmer in 1918 to be the standard German light tank. It weighed 8.75 tons, carried a crew of three, was armed with a 57mm Nordenfelt or 37m Krupp main gun, and had armor ranging from 8 to 14mm. Parts for ten of these quite advanced vehicles were smuggled to Sweden in 1921, where five of them were rebuilt as the M21 with two machine guns in a fully rotating turret, and the remaining five modified as M29s, by mounting a 37mm main gun, also in a rotating turret.

After his trip to Sweden, Guderian's ideas about armored troops entered their final phase. He concluded that tanks should be employed in armored divisions and that these armored divisions should be balanced combined-arms formations, including reconnaissance elements; support troops, which were transported in tracked armored vehicles; and organic artillery capable of cross-country movement. This idea was not wholly attributable to Guderian, as the combined-arms concept, which included air support, was common throughout the German Army due to von Seeckt's early influence. Continuing this train of thought, however, Guderian desired seeing panzer divisions concentrated into armored corps, thus moving his concepts from the tactical to the operational realm. He wanted not only a breakthrough weapon, but also the ability to move beyond the front lines and enjoy operational success.

For command and control, Guderian was also a proponent of the widespread use of radios, down to the individual tank. Although it was not always possible to install radio receivers and transmitters in all tanks initially, this farsighted measure helped insure a large German tactical advantage in the first three years of the war.

Along with *Hauptmann* Pirner, an ordnance officer, Guderian envisaged two main types of tank: a light tank with an armor-piercing main gun and two machine guns, and a medium tank with a heavier-caliber gun, probably of 75mm caliber, and two machine guns. The maximum weight of the tanks was to be 24 tons, due to the carrying capacity of German bridges, and they were to be able to attain a maximum speed of 40kph. The proposed organization of a tank battalion was three companies of light tanks and one company of medium ones, with the medium tanks engaging targets out of range of the light tanks.

Guderian wanted a 50mm gun for the light tank in order to defeat the heavier armor that was starting to appear on some foreign tanks. In that respect he was overruled, as the Army Ordnance Office and Inspector of Artillery stipulated a 37mm gun since the infantry was in the process of being equipped with 37mm antitank guns.

In 1932 exercises were held with reinforced infantry regiments, tank battalions equipped with dummy tanks, and armored cars based on six-wheel commercial truck chassis. These early motorized and armored operations were considered very successful, demonstrating the considerable potential of independent armored formations.

In 1933 Adolf Hitler became chancellor of Germany. With him, General von Blomberg became the war minister and General von Reichenau the chief of the Ministerial Office. Both of these generals favored the creation of an armored force. Even the chief of the General Staff, General Beck, was not the impediment to the development of panzer divisions, as is often claimed, although he did advocate the formation of armored brigades to support the infantry divisions. At a demonstration for Hitler at Kummersdorf in 1934, Guderian demonstrated a motorcycle platoon, an antitank platoon, a platoon of preproduction *Panzer I* light tanks, a platoon of light armored cars (*Kfz. 13*), and a platoon of heavy six-wheel armored cars (*Sd.Kfz. 231*). The speed and precision of the formation markedly impressed Hitler, who remarked: "That's what I need! That's what I want to have!"

It would be incorrect to attribute the creation of the panzer forces primarily to the National Socialist government, as this was well under way prior to 1933. The repudiation of the Versailles Treaty on March 16, 1935, and subsequent rearmament of the armed forces certainly accelerated the process. By the time the Nazis took power, however, the basic structure of the panzer division and the fundamental design parameters of German tanks were already in place.

***

The initial *Panzer I*, the *Ausführung A ohne Aufbau,* was designated as an agricultural tractor to disguise its true purpose. Fifteen of these turretless vehicles were produced by five manufacturing firms (three each) in early 1934. Intended as a training vehicle, they were issued to the first two panzer regiments to give the troops the much-needed experience of driving and maintaining a fully tracked armored vehicle.

The first armed *Panzer I*, the *Ausführung A,* with twin 7.92mm *MG13* machine guns in a fully rotating turret, were produced from July 1934 to June 1936, with 818 being manufactured. By July 1935, 475 had been received by the armored vehicle training command. Although never intended as a combat vehicle, the *Panzer I* nevertheless saw extensive service in the campaigns in Poland, France, Norway, and the Low Countries. As with most German armored vehicles, it also saw extensive service after being repurposed as a self-propelled antitank gun and self-propelled heavy infantry gun, among other service and support roles.

The *Panzer II*, with its 20mm automatic cannon capable of firing both armor-piercing and high-explosive rounds, was first produced in May 1936, with 75 of the *Ausführung a* (preproduction version) being delivered by February 1937. Twenty-five of the extensively modified *Ausführung b* were produced in February and March 1937, with both variants issued to panzer units starting that spring. A total of 1,113 vehicles were produced from March 1937 to April 1940. These included the final preproduction model, the *Ausführung c,* as well as the first three variants of the production series, the *A, B,* and *C.*

After 1940 the *Panzer II* was used primarily as a reconnaissance vehicle in the light tank platoons of the panzer regiment headquarters. The generally robust chassis was used as a self-propelled antitank gun with the *76mm Pak 36(r)* and *75mm Pak 40*, with nearly 900 vehicles converted/produced in that role. Starting in February 1943, all *Panzer II* chassis were used for the production of the very effective *Sd.Kfz. 124 Wespe* (Wasp) self-propelled light field howitzer mounting the *105mm leichte Feldhaubitze 18M*. In all, 676 were produced until July 1944, along with 159 munitions carriers.

The *Panzer III* was first produced in 1937, but only 42 were in service by March 1938. The *Panzer III* was beginning to be phased out as a main battle tank in late 1943. However, the *Panzer III* chassis was produced almost until the end of the war as the *Sturmgeschütz III/40* and the *Sturmhaubitze 42* (with a 105mm assault howitzer).

The *Panzer IV* was likewise first produced in October 1937 and kept in production until March 1945, being progressively up-armored and up-gunned. Even at the end of the war, the venerable *Panzer IV* could still give a reasonably good account of itself against most medium Allied and Soviet tanks. By August 1939 only a total of 211 of the *Panzer IV, Ausführung A, B,* and *C,* had been produced. The *Panzer IV* chassis was eventually utilized in such diverse roles as an assault gun, tank destroyer, self-propelled artillery gun, and self-propelled antiaircraft gun.

In addition, it was recognized early in the development of the panzer divisions that the infantry and artillery need to keep pace with the fully tracked tanks. Accordingly, an entire family of excellent half-tracked vehicles were developed to fill that role, beginning in 1937. The 1-ton and 3-ton *Zugkraftwagen* (artillery tractor) formed the basis for the light (*Sd.Kfz. 250*) and medium (*Sd.Kfz. 251*) armored carriers, respectively, both entering service in small numbers in 1939. These very adaptable vehicles were produced in numerous variants, 12 for the *Sd.Kfz. 250* and 23 for the *Sd.Kfz. 251*, with over 6,600 (*250*) and 15,250 (*251*) produced. The *Sd.Kfz. 251* was the most-produced German armored fighting vehicle of the war. However, due to Germany's limited industrial base, there were never enough of these vehicles to meet the constant demand.

***

In 1934 General Lutz was appointed commander of the newly established Armored Troops Command with *Oberst* Guderian as his chief of staff, a position where he could influence the future development of all aspects of the armored force. The first exercise with the initial panzer division took place at Lüneburg Heath in August 1935 under the scrutiny of the army commander in chief, General von Fritsch. During the exercise, von Fritsch ordered the panzer division to make a 90-degree turn in order to confront an attack on its flank and, despite a lack of training and scarcity of radios, it only took the division about 90 minutes to adjust to the unexpected situation and mount a successful counterattack. The senior officers present were uniformly impressed by this demonstration of flexibility and speed.

In October 1935 the three panzer divisions that had been approved in 1934 were established. They were composed of two tank regiments, each of two battalions; one motorized infantry regiment of two battalions; one battalion of motorcyclists; one battalion of armored reconnaissance vehicles; an artillery regiment; an antitank battalion; a combat engineer battalion; and integral maintenance and logistical supporting elements.

Guderian was given command of the *2. Panzer-Division*, a position he held from October 15, 1935, to February 4, 1938, being promoted to *Generalmajor* in August 1936. In Guderian's opinion, this command somewhat prevented him from extending his influence to the armed forces in general, particularly in relation to the establishment of panzer brigades to support the infantry divisions and light divisions that were a concession to the cavalry, although he may have been overestimating his influence. Nonetheless, it gave him valuable command experience.

In 1938 Guderian published *Achtung! Panzer!*, a book that provided an overview of the development of armor and its role in the Great War, armor's postwar developments, and, most importantly, his theories regarding the ideal structure of armored divisions, their role in combat, and their mass employment in separate panzer corps. Well regarded in German military circles, the book appeared to be largely ignored outside Germany. A careful reading by the foreign military would have revealed the basic concept of the *Blitzkrieg* that so surprised all opposing armies in the early years of the war.

In February 1938 Guderian relinquished command of the *2. Panzer-Division,* and assumed command of the *XVI. Armee-Korps (mot)*, and was promoted to *Generalleutnant*. As part of the forces involved in the annexation of Austria in March 1938, Guderian's corps was given control of the *2. Panzer-Division* and Hitler's elite guard, the motorized *SS-Leibstandarte*. The formations involved gained valuable experience in the difficulties encountered on long road marches. Despite some claims to the contrary, the march generally went well, although there were some logistical problems with maintenance and refueling that were immediately attended to.

In September 1938 Hitler took the risk of ordering the occupation of part of Czechoslovakia, the ethnically German *Sudetenland*, on the flimsiest of pretexts. This also involved a long-distance movement of armored elements. Once again, the operation was essentially an exercise in administrative movement, since the occupation was not opposed by the Czechs. When the rest of the country was occupied in March 1939, the German Army acquired a first-rate armaments industry and swiftly incorporated two excellent vehicles, the *Panzer 35(t)* and *Panzer 38(t)*, into its tank inventory.

In roughly the same period, some *Panzer I* tanks were sent to Spain during its civil war. Germany supported the nationalist forces of General Franco against the left-wing Republicans. The experience gained with these vehicles played virtually no part in the development of tank tactics, other than to demonstrate that the *Panzer I* was almost totally useless as a combat-capable vehicle.

On November 20, 1938, Guderian was appointed Commander of Mobile Troops, incorporating panzer divisions, motorized infantry, light divisions, and cavalry, with the rank of *General der Panzertruppe.* He immediately set to work producing training manuals for the panzer troops, as none existed at the time. When the German armed forces were mobilized on August 22, 1939, Guderian became the commanding general of the newly formed *XIX. Armee-Korps (mot),* which comprised the *3. Panzer Division*, the *2. Infanterie-Division (mot)*, and the *3. Infanterie-Division (mot)*, in addition to corps troops. This was Guderian's command on the eve of war.

ABOVE: The most commonly seen tank of the prewar years was the *Panzerkampfwagen I,* which predominated due to the sheer numbers produced compared to other prewar German armor. In the first image, *Panzerkampfwagen I*s of an unknown unit are seen moving down a street in the town of Neuhammer, which was adjacent to the training area of the same name in prewar Silesia (present-day Poland). Since most of the early vehicles did not have radio communications, hand-and-arm signals, occasionally augmented by signal disks such as these, were used to conduct unit movement and maneuver. These signal devices consisted of a red-and-white-painted metal disc attached to a short wooden handle. Note that the three-digit vehicle numbers are painted in white on the front armor of each tank. The famous German national insignia, the *Balkenkreuz* (beamed [timbered] cross), was generally not seen on these early vehicles. (MICHAEL H. PRUETT)

LEFT: In another period postcard, we see an early variant of the *Panzer I* on maneuvers at an undisclosed training area. This tank shows evidence of the three-tone camouflage pattern described earlier, along with sprayed black lines separating the camouflage colors. (MICHAEL H. PRUETT)

TOP: Spotless examples of German armor can be seen on display at the German Automotive Exposition of 1938. A *Panzer I* takes pride of place behind the *Gefreiter* standing guard, while two examples of armored cars bring up the rear, the *Sd.Kfz. 221* and the *Sd.Kfz. 231 (8-Rad)*. Like the *Panzer I*, the *Sd.Kfz. 221* was essentially obsolete by the start of the war, although it continued to be used in armored reconnaissance battalions as late as 1942. Its thin armor and single 7.92mm machine gun were no match for Soviet weaponry on the Eastern Front. The larger armored car, the eight-wheeled *Sd.Kfz. 231*, had a longer service life and examples were still in use by war's end, although they had largely been replaced by the *Sd.Kfz. 234* family of heavy armored cars and other reconnaissance vehicles by then. The two-tone camouflage consisting of dark brown and dark gray can clearly be seen on the *Sd.Kfz. 221*. (MICHAEL H. PRUETT)

BOTTOM: A motor pool bay showing the assets of a headquarters section of a panzer regiment. In the foreground is a *Panzer I*, followed by at least six command versions of the tank, the *Panzerbefehlswagen I*, and then several light armored cars and an *Sd.Kfz. 232* or, more unlikely, *263 (6-Rad)*. Headquarters staff cars make up the second row, as well as motorcycles for the messenger section. The two-tone prewar camouflage pattern can be seen on many of the tactical vehicles. Some 190 *Panzerbefehlswagen I* command vehicles were produced between 1935 and 1937. They were based on the chassis of the *B* version of the *Panzer I*, which was longer than the *A* version. It had a more powerful engine (100 horsepower versus 60 horsepower) and more fuel capacity. That said, it was still extremely cramped for a command and control vehicle and was soon replaced by other armored vehicles, generally the *Panzerbefehlswagen III*, with many of the older command vehicles being converted into armored ambulances. (MICHAEL H. PRUETT)

ABOVE: A period photo postcard showing a *Panzerkampfwagen II* as it negotiates a ditch. The *Panzer II* was also never intended to be a front-line combat vehicle but, like the *Panzer I*, it saw extensive service in the initial stages of World War II as a tank and until the end of the war in a variety of other roles. Some 100 preproduction models were produced (as the *Ausführung a1/a2/a3, b,* and *c*) before series production commenced in 1937 with the *Ausführung A*. By the time the *C* version finished production in April 1940, more than 1,000 vehicles had been manufactured. Armed with a 2cm automatic cannon and a coaxial 7.92mm machine gun, the *Panzer II* was adequate in the initial campaigns of the war, but it was severely put to the test when employed against the Soviet Union in 1941. Later versions featured differing types of roadwheel and suspension design in addition to features such as upgraded power plants and armament as well as operational employment (e.g., the combat engineer flamethrower vehicle or fully tracked armored reconnaissance vehicle). Like the *Panzer I*, many *Panzer II*s found an extended service life by serving as the conversion basis for self-propelled guns, self-propelled antitank guns, combat engineer bridge layers, armored ammunition carriers, and driver-training vehicles. (MICHAEL H. PRUETT)

FACING PAGE: These *Panzer II, Ausführung a* preproduction vehicles later had their turrets removed and were relegated to duties in the training base as instructional vehicles for driver training. The suspension on these preproduction vehicles differed substantially from the production series. (PERIOD LITERATURE VIA MICHAEL H. PRUETT)

ABOVE AND FACING PAGE: During the prewar period, armored cavalry divisions were envisioned as a doctrinal partner with the armored divisions and were intended to serve as a sort of long-range reconnaissance asset of the armored force. The light divisions (*leichte Divisionen*), of which there were four, proved to be of limited value after their employment in Poland. They were found to be too lightly armored and vulnerable to a determined foe and were converted to armored divisions before the invasion of France. Part of the mobility of a light division was to come from its battalion of tanks, which were to be truck-transported to the front before being operationally deployed, thus saving wear and tear on the tracked assets.

These three images come from a prewar publication, which extolled the virtues of the light divisions. They are most likely of *Panzer-Abteilung 65* of the *1. leichte Division*. As can be seen from the three pictures, one truck was responsible for the transport of two tanks, with one riding on the open cargo bed of the truck itself and the other transported via a trailer. In the remaining images, the *Ausführung D* and *Ausführung E* of the *Panzer II*, which were specially produced for just this role and had a radically different suspension with only four large roadwheels and no return rollers, can be seen during a military parade and preparations for loading them on the specially designed trailers. The trailer being used is the *Tiefladeanhänger für Panzerkampfwagen (Sonderanhänger 115)*, and the truck is a standard heavy commercial truck of the period. Generally, the trucks were either the Büssing-NAG *Typ 900* or the Faun *L900*. (PERIOD LITERATURE VIA MICHAEL H. PRUETT)

ABOVE: With the annexation of Czechoslovakia in March 1939 came numerous spoils for the German Army, including the Skoda works, which had produced armored vehicles for the Czechoslovak Army. The two primary armored vehicles, the *Lehký tank vzor 35* (Light Tank Model 35) and the *Lehký tank vzor 38* (Light Tank Model 38), were incorporated into the *Panzertruppe* as the *Panzer 35(t)* and the *Panzer 38(t)*. About 200 *Panzer 35(t)*s saw service with the Germans until around 1942—primarily with *Panzer-Regiment 11* of the *6. Panzer-Division*—when the remaining operational tanks were scrapped or sold to Romania. It was armed with a 37mm main gun and two 7.92mm machine guns. Enjoying substantially more operational success was the *Panzer 38(t),* of which more than 1,400 served the Germans. It also had a 37mm main gun and two 7.92mm machine guns, but it was considerably superior automotively. Although tank production ceased in 1942, the chassis continued to be manufactured and was used for antitank gun designs (around 1,500 *Marder III*s and 2,800 *Hetzer*s), antiaircraft gun carriers (about 140), and fully tracked armored reconnaissance vehicles (around 70).

FACING PAGE TOP: The *Panzer 38(t)* in German service, as reflected by this period photo postcard. (POSTCARD VIA MICHAEL H. PRUETT)

FACING PAGE, BOTTOM TWO: This *Panzer 38(t),* possibly an *Ausführung A,* is seen in a motor pool in Bielefeld, the home base of *Panzer-Regiment 11.* In the second image, which is double exposed, it can be seen that the coaxial machine gun has been removed from the turret. (MICHAEL H. PRUETT)

FACING PAGE: The *Panzer III* was originally conceived to be Germany's main battle tank, and its development history goes back to 1934. Initial variants, of which the *A* model is seen here, saw a variety of suspension designs until the familiar six-roadwheel and three-return-roller version was introduced with the *Ausführung E* in 1939. Although the *A* to *D* variants should be considered pre-production models, a number of them were manufactured and even saw combat, at least through the campaign in the West in 1940: *Ausführung A*, 10 tanks; *Ausführung B,* 10; *Ausführung C*, 15; and *Ausführung D,* 30. Production of the *Panzer III* ended with the *N* version in 1943, after slightly more than 5,500 tanks of all production variants had been produced. Like its sister tanks, the *Panzer I* and the *Panzer II*, the vehicle also served as a command and control vehicle (nearly 400) and an armored combat engineer vehicle (flamethrower) (100). In addition, it served as the basis for the most familiar German assault gun, the *Sturmgeschütz III*, which was produced until the end of the war.

The *Panzer III* started service life with a 37mm main gun, which later became a 50mm cannon of increasingly longer length. The final combat version of the tank had a short-barreled 75mm main gun of 24 calibers, thus assuming an infantry support role or, in the case of the *Tiger* battalions, an escort role in an effort to keep infantry hunter/killer teams from approaching the heavy tanks. The *Panzer III* was the first German tank with a three-man turret, a design feature that was kept in all subsequent German tank designs. While the *Panzer III* served well early in the war, it rapidly reached obsolescence in the demanding cauldron of the Eastern Front.

This *Panzer III, Ausführung A,* negotiates an obstacle during trials. The *A* is easily identified by its five large roadwheels and two return rollers. In addition to its 37mm main gun, it had three 7.92mm machine guns, two coaxially mounted with the main gun and one in a hull mount. Production versions of the tank only had one coaxial machine gun.

BELOW: Another view of the *Panzer III, Ausführung A,* during trials. Both images come from period postcards designed to show the power of the newly created *Panzertruppe.*

ABOVE: Not generally realized is the fact that Germany's armored forces started with the concurrent buildup of armored reconnaissance elements, since it was easier to circumvent the restrictions placed on Germany by the Versailles Treaty with wheeled armed and armored vehicles. Each of the armored divisions and motorized infantry divisions was authorized a motorized reconnaissance battalion, which had at least one armored car troop as part of its organization. The prewar light divisions had large complements of armored cars, and even some of the prewar line infantry divisions were authorized at least an armored car platoon. As with the development of tanks, German industry was never able to keep up with demand, and the German Army entered (and ended) the war with a number of designs that were obsolescent before they even saw their first combat.

In this image, an armored mock-up of the early 1930s *Reichswehr* makes its way down a road during maneuvers. Vehicles such as these provided the training upon which the wartime leaders of Germany's armored forces were developed. The initial armored cars of the *Reichswehr*, the *Kfz. 13* and *Kfz. 14*, were both adaptations of existing civilian vehicles.

FACING PAGE TOP: The armored scout troop of an unknown reconnaissance battalion stages in an open field during prewar maneuvers. A significant number of armored cars available to the prewar armored reconnaissance forces can be seen in this image, ranging from the *Sd.Kfz. 232 (6-Rad)* in the foreground to the *Sd.Kfz. 231 (6-Rad)* (behind the *232*s) to the *Sd.Kfz. 221* (viewer's left) to the *Kfz. 13 "Adler"* (in the center next to the initial row of trucks). The six-wheeled *Sd.Kfz. 231*s and *232*s were the first heavy armored cars to see service for reconnaissance purposes. Like most German armored-car designs of the period, the vehicles were not purpose-built for the envisioned role but were conversions based on the chassis of existing civilian designs. Both vehicles were armed with a 20mm semiautomatic cannon and a coaxial 7.92mm machine gun, and the radio version—the *232*—featured a 100-watt radio. Only 123 of the vehicles were built from 1932 to 1935, but some saw service in the initial campaigns of World War II. The *Sd.Kfz. 221* was also obsolete prior to the start of the war, but vehicles were in front-line service in reconnaissance battalions until 1943, due to the perennial shortage of armed vehicles in the German armed forces. The vehicle was armed with a single 7.92mm machine gun in a revolving turret and had limited protection against small-arms fire. Some models were later equipped with antitank rifles of varying calibers. It performed well in the initial campaigns of the war, but its limited cross-country mobility and light armor proved to be its undoing in the harsh environment of the Soviet Union. Finally, the *Kfz. 13* was the first "armored car" used by the fledgling motorized reconnaissance forces. It was a reconfigured civilian Adler touring car with an open top and a 7.92mm machine gun on a pedestal mount. It actually saw front-line service into 1940, although primarily with the armored car platoons of infantry divisions.

ABOVE: The heavy sections of an armored-car scout troop line up for inspection prior to the start of prewar maneuvers. The officer with the white bands around his sleeves is an "umpire" for the event. A lone *Sd.Kfz. 221* is parked off to the side, perhaps serving as an umpire vehicle (see the additional officer with white armbands behind the vehicle).

FACING PAGE TOP: In another prewar maneuver image, two heavy sections of a scout platoon move down an unimproved road. In this case, it appears that an apparent lack of vehicles has forced the pairing of a *Kfz. 13* with an *Sd.Kfz. 232 (6-Rad)* to form the second heavy section, an unusual combination.

FACING PAGE BOTTOM: Scouts wash their vehicles in a stream, most likely before they return to their garrison after a maneuver. The *Sd.Kfz. 231 (6-Rad)* to the viewer's left has had its weaponry dismounted. In front of it is an *Sd.Kfz. 223*, a hybrid between the *Sd.Kfz. 222* (chassis) and *Sd.Kfz. 221* (turret), which had a collapsible bed-frame antenna and both medium- and long-range radio sets. These were seen in service until war's end and produced from 1935 through January 1944, with 550 being manufactured. An *Sd.Kfz. 231 (8-Rad)* is seen on the viewer's right. It gradually replaced the six-wheeled *Sd.Kfz. 231* in the late 1930s and some were seen in service until war's end, with a total of more than 1,200 having been manufactured. Likes its predecessor, it had two drivers, one facing the front and one facing the rear, with the ability to quickly engage in either position, allowing the vehicle an unprecedented ability to withdraw quickly when it was in danger of revealing its position or being engaged.

BELOW: Another view of heavy armored cars from the *Reichswehr* era, as seen in a period postcard. (PERIOD LITERATURE VIA MICHAEL H. PRUETT)

ABOVE AND FACING PAGE: Several views of heavy armored radio cars, which were used to facilitate communications between scouts out front and divisional headquarters, usually relatively far to the rear. The earlier version of the radio car, the *Sd.Kfz. 263 (6-Rad)*, is often hard to distinguish from the *Sd.Kfz. 232 (6-Rad)*, with which it bears a very close resemblance. On close inspection, the radio version can be determined by looking at the mounting poles for the bed-frame antenna. Two poles on the sides of the turret and near its front prevent it from traversing, a hallmark of the radio car. In this image, we see an *Sd.Kfz. 263 (6-Rad)* attributed to the reconnaissance battalion of the *7. Panzer-Division*, *Aufklärungs-Abteilung 37 (mot)*.

FACING PAGE TOP: Another view of an *Sd.Kfz. 263 (6-Rad)* attributed to the same battalion. The vertical object encased in the tarpaulin on the turret roof is the mount for the mast antenna, which could be erected when the vehicle was in static positions to increase radio range even further.

FACING PAGE BOTTOM: The later version of the radio car was the *Sd.Kfz. 263 (8-Rad),* which had a production run of 240 vehicles before the last one was manufactured in January 1943. This *Sd.Kfz. 263 (8-Rad)* is attributed to *Aufklärungs-Abteilung 5 (mot)* of the *2. Panzer-Division*. Of interest is the fitting of snow chains and the mounting of a good-luck charm—a horseshoe—on the front slope of the vehicle. The turret of the earlier vehicle was replaced by a large, boxy superstructure, which allowed for a roomier work environment and the use of map boards.

The old and the newer. Prewar maneuvers pass through a small German town, where armored reconnaissance forces at a halt observe bicycle and horse-mounted troops. Since most of the armored reconnaissance scouts originally came from cavalry elements, there is probably some wistfulness on their part. The vehicles appear to have been painted in the two-tone camouflage of the later 1930s, as evidenced by the rather stark contrast on the spare tire covers on the *Kfz. 13* and the *Sd.Kfz. 232 (6-Rad)*. An *Sd.Kfz. 221* leads the column of vehicles. (PERIOD LITERATURE VIA MICHAEL H. PRUETT)

An atmospheric shot of an *Sd.Kfz. 232 (6-Rad)*, attributed to *Aufklärungs-Abteilung 5 (mot)*, coordinating with other elements on a road.

A heavy section consisting of an *Sd.Kfz. 231 (6-Rad)* and an *Sd.Kfz. 232 (6-Rad)* conducts cross-country maneuvers. The staff car in between the two armored cars was probably for a maneuver observer or umpire.

ABOVE, BOTH: Prewar training for all members of the *Panzertruppe* was rigorous, thorough, and demanding and followed the adage *Schweiß spart Blut!* (Sweat spares blood!). Such training helped instill confidence and instinctive reactions to actual combat situations. Artificial smoke was often used to help mask a withdrawal under enemy observation or fire.

TOP: The vehicle commander of an *Sd.Kfz. 231 (8-Rad)* observes a wire obstacle during training. This was probably a staged image, since scouts would normally dismount to examine a wire obstacle placed before a bridge entrance, especially since it was expected that the enemy would also cover the obstacle, or place observed fire on it.

BOTTOM: An *Sd.Kfz. 232 (6-Rad)* moves through a minor water obstacle in high country during prewar maneuvers. (FINAL THREE IMAGES FROM PERIOD LITERATURE VIA MICHAEL H. PRUETT)

RIGHT: A lineup of armored cars at Krampnitz, the home of the German Army's reconnaissance school. First in line is an *Sd.Kfz. 231 (8-Rad)*, followed by an *Sd.Kfz. 232 (8-Rad)*, an *Sd.Kfz. 222*, and an *Sd.Kfz. 221*. A three-tone camouflage can be seen to good advantage on the lead vehicle.

BELOW: In the second image, also taken at Krampnitz, *Sd.Kfz. 222*s are lined up with weapons elevated in an antiaircraft defensive mode. The *Sd.Kfz. 222* was one of the more successful armored car designs, with around 1,800 being manufactured in seven minor variations from 1936 to 1943. Like its heavier counterparts, the *Sd.Kfz. 222* mounted a 20mm semiautomatic cannon in a fully traversing turret that also featured a 7.92mm coaxial machine gun. (PERIOD LITERATURE VIA MICHAEL H. PRUETT)

The *Panzertruppe* gained a lot of practical experience during the prewar occupations of Austria, the Sudetenland, and then the remainder of Czechoslovakia. In this image, scouts from an unidentified reconnaissance element take a break along a road. An *Sd.Kfz. 223* is in the foreground, while an *Sd.Kfz. 222* is parked behind it. The presence of flowers on the vehicles indicates that this image was probably taken during the occupation of Austria in 1938, where the Germans were greeted in an overwhelmingly friendly manner.

This *Sd.Kfz. 231 (8-Rad)* has parked alongside the road in a small German village during maneuvers. The vehicle was most likely assigned to *Aufklärungs-Abteilung 8 (mot)* of the *5. Panzer-Division*, as indicated by the tactical insignia—a stylized armored car with the numeral 8 on it—barely visible under the right rear muffler. Not only were all eight wheels on the armored car capable of steering, but they all turned at slightly different angles, thus considerably shortening the turning radius of the vehicle.

FACING PAGE TOP: A *Kfz. 13* and *Aufklärungs-Abteilung 8 (mot)* scout pulls security duty at a harbor where the *Aviso Grille*, the official German state yacht, is docked.

FACING PAGE BOTTOM: *Aufklärungs-Abteilung 8 (mot)* scouts wait for their train to pull out after having loaded their *Kfz. 13*s onto railcars. Rail movement was always the preferred method to transport tactical vehicles over longer distances in an effort to reduce wear and tear.

TOP: *Aufklärungs-Abteilung 8 (mot)* scouts pose for comrades and prepare their vehicles for gunnery training at the ranges at Stahnsdorf. An *Sd.Kfz. 222* in pristine condition serves as a backdrop for an informal pose. The scouts are all wearing the early version of the panzer tunic, which featured wide lapels, a smaller collar with branch-of-service piping (*Waffenfarbe*) and Death's Head collar tabs, and shoulder straps. In addition, the unit of assignment was sewn into the shoulder straps on junior enlisted personnel using the appropriate *Waffenfarbe*. This practice was eliminated during the war years as an operational security measure.

BOTTOM: Magazines for the 20mm semiautomatic cannon on the *Sd.Kfz. 222* are loaded on the cargo bed of a truck. The two scouts sitting on the cargo-bed benches have 20mm rounds in their hands.

ABOVE: Scouts strike a relaxed pose in front of an armored car, while other scouts continue to load magazines in the truck to the rear.

RIGHT: A more serious pose is struck in the final image from this series.

ABOVE: The next three images are period photo postcards that were purchased by a scout assigned to *Panzer-Aufklärungs-Ausbildung- und Ersatz-Abteilung 4* in Sondershausen. In the first image, an *Sd.Kfz. 232 (6-Rad)* moves down a cobblestone lane, followed by an *Sd.Kfz. 221.* The lead vehicle is the sixth vehicle in the scout troop's heavy section, as indicated by the letter *F* on the hull sides and front slope. Typically vehicles were also christened with a name or phrase that began with its letter. In this case, it is *Frisch darauf und durch*, meaning "Boldly on and through." The prewar three-tone camouflage can be seen to good advantage, as well as the stylized armored car used to mark the vehicle. The back side of this particular postcard contains the written words *mein Panzer* (my tank). It is not known whether this was meant to indicate this was the actual vehicle to which the scout was assigned or simply an indicator that he was assigned to that type of vehicle.

FACING PAGE TOP: Two six-wheeled armored cars move down an unimproved road, with the trail vehicle definitely being an *Sd.Kfz. 263 (6-Rad)*, a vehicle produced in very small numbers. In addition to the *Wehrmacht* license plates seen on each mudguard, the tactical marking for the armored reconnaissance battalion can also be seen above the license plate on the left side. The early camouflage scheme is visible on the spare-tire cover.

FACING PAGE BOTTOM: A heavy section is seen on a dirt trail at what appears to be training grounds. The lead vehicle, an *Sd.Kfz. 231 (6-Rad)*, has a cloth camouflage cover over its license plate, an effort to hide the vehicle's signature from enemy observation.

FACING PAGE TOP: The prewar *Panzertruppe* also envisioned the use of "fast troops" mounted primarily on motorcycles and motorcycle/sidecar combinations. Because of their speed, the *Kradschützen* were incorporated into motorized reconnaissance battalions as a company-sized element and existed as separate motorcycle infantry battalions, which were found in motorized infantry divisions and armor divisions. The latter often worked in tandem with the divisional reconnaissance assets, especially when pulling guard, screen, and economy-of-force missions. While speed worked to the advantage of the *Kradschützen* in the early campaigns, their lack of armor protection, poor cross-country mobility, and dearth of "boots on the ground" led to their gradual (theoretical) elimination by 1943 and incorporation of remaining assets into reconnaissance battalions.

In this image, motorcycle infantry conduct prewar river-crossing exercises on an engineered pontoon boat. Like scout elements, the *Kradschützen* had no organic means by which to cross water obstacles. They had to find intact bridges or fords or use bridging assets provided by combat engineers. Efforts were made later in the war to provide a modicum of amphibious capability—e.g., the *Volkswagen Schwimmwagen* or the Trippel amphibian—but the success of those efforts was limited.

FACING PAGE BOTTOM: *Kradschützen* practice maneuvers under difficult conditions. The limitations of the motorcycle infantry came to the fore during the campaign against the Soviet Union, where an improved road network was practically nonexistent and harsh weather severely limited their mobility. While the wheel on some sidecars was also powered, the additional mobility was not enough to overcome the general disadvantages encountered there.

BELOW AND FOLOWING PAGES: The following images all come from a photo album kept by a scout assigned to the reconnaissance troop of the prewar *Leibstandarte*, which later evolved into one of the most famous German armored formations of the war, the *1. SS-Panzer-Division "Leibstandarte SS Adolf Hitler"* (*LAH*). Contrary to popular belief, the *Leibstandarte* did not even start to have tanks within its table of organization and equipment until 1942. Until then the formation's only armored assets were within the various reconnaissance elements assigned to it, starting with a platoon in the mid-1930s and gradually becoming a battalion-sized element by the outbreak of the war. These *Sd.Kfz. 221*s appear to be among the first armored cars issued to the *Leibstandarte* and can be seen in the motor pool and on a winter road march.

ABOVE: In this image, the *Sd.Kfz. 221*s can be seen with their weapons mounted for the first time. The officer (on the viewer's right), an *SS-Obersturmführer* (1st lieutenant), is probably the platoon leader, while the noncommissioned officer, an *SS-Oberscharführer*, is most likely the platoon sergeant. The image is highly interesting from a uniform perspective, inasmuch as the *SS* (*Schutzstaffel* or protective service) scouts are wearing army uniforms pressed into *SS* service. The collar tabs are piped in an unknown *Waffenfarbe*, which appears to stand in stark contrast to the rose-pink *Waffenfarbe* that is piped around the collars. The NCO's shoulder straps appear to be of the standard enlisted variety of the time, featuring the oversize *LAH* cipher. They both wear the army beret/crash helmet combination, to which the stylized *SS* skull and oversize *SS* eagles have been applied.

RIGHT: This scout sits astride a motorcycle/sidecar combination, which features the unit designation, a stylized armored car with *17. LAH* (*17. Kompanie* of the *Leibstandarte*).

THIS PAGE AND FACING PAGE: The *Leibstandarte* appears to have just received its *Sd.Kfz. 232*s (and *Sd.Kfz. 231*s) in these images, judging by the pristine condition of the vehicles. They are seen at an unknown gunnery range. The officer seen previously is visible in the second image, lying on the rear deck and talking to the crew through the open rear hatch.

ABOVE: *SS* scouts take time from working on their vehicles in the field to strike a casual pose.

FACING PAGE: These *SS* scouts strike a martial pose in front of their *Sd.Kfz. 231* and *232 (8-Rad)* vehicles. The majority of the scouts appear to still have piping around their collar tabs and oversize ciphers on their shoulder straps, features that would disappear by the start of the war.

TOP: The reconnaissance elements line up in a field motor pool located on a soccer field, probably during training or maneuvers of some sort. The tactical vehicles seem to have their weaponry mounted beneath the protective tarpaulins. The left-hand *Sd.Kfz. 232 (8-Rad)* shows evidence of the prewar two-tone camouflage pattern, while it is almost impossible to discern on its sister vehicle to the right. Of interest are the stylized tactical markings for an armored reconnaissance element, as well as the christening of the two heavy armored cars (*Casella* and *Faust*).

BOTTOM: Elements of the *Leibstandarte*'s reconnaissance troop line up for crossing the border into Austria in March 1938.

THIS PAGE AND NEXT PAGE: The commander of the *Leibstandarte,* Josef "Sepp" Dietrich, greets his forces at the border, which has been marked with a sign saying *Wie alle gehören dem Führer!* (All of us belong to the *Führer*!). In the next four images, *Sd.Kfz. 232 (8-Rad)* armored cars cross the barrier at the frontier, while a large crowd observes the event. In both instances a large *Balkenkreuz* adorns the front slope of the vehicles.

LEFT: *SS* scouts strike a martial pose during a rest halt. The scout on the viewer's far right can be seen in a relatively famous photograph being decorated by Dietrich after the fall of France in 1940.

AVOVE AND RIGHT: Most of the armored cars have pulled over to the side of the road and formed a cordon in anticipation of Hitler following the *Sd.Kfz. 221* seen in the first image. Hitler moves past the honor cordon, with the *SS* scouts saluting as he passes.

Final images from the occupation, with another view of Dietrich, seen here wearing his Great War awards, including the Tank Assault Badge.

Of vital importance to fast-moving and wide-ranging armor operations were reliable, far-reaching radio communications. In order to keep up with tanks, armor regiments and divisions were provided with sections of armored signals assets, such as those seen here, parked in a German town square. Leading the lineup is an *Sd.Kfz. 263 (8-Rad)*. It is followed by several light armored radio cars, either the *Sd.Kfz. 260* or the *Sd.Kfz. 261*, with the former having a mast antenna and the latter a bed-frame antenna. Bringing up the rear is a *Panzer III*, possibly a *Panzerbefehlswagen III*, which served as a command and control vehicle for the regiment.

FACING PAGE TOP: Although radio communications were paramount within armored commands, landlines and wire communications were the preferred method of communicating when in static defensive positions and staging areas. To that end, "wire dogs," such as these signals soldiers, worked tirelessly to lay and retrieve wire as the situation demanded. Wire was often placed in tree limbs to avoid being torn up by vehicular traffic on the ground.

FACING PAGE BOTTOM: Assigned to a *Luftwaffe FlaK* unit, this Büssing-NAG *Typ G31* truck is employed laying communications cable. Note the red-and-white hand-signal disc and the step assist mounted on the tailgate of the truck. (MICHAEL H. PRUETT)

BELOW: Each panzer and motorized/mechanized division had a medical company in support. Although front-line forces sometimes had the luxury of a half or fully tracked vehicle for the evacuation of the wounded, the most common method of evacuation was on trucks such as these, the Mercedes-Benz *Typ L3000S*. The Red Cross emblem appears on both fenders and on the canvas cover. For some unexplained reason, the driver wears the national emblem and Red Cross armband but lacks both collar tabs and shoulder straps on his field service tunic! (MICHAEL H. PRUETT)

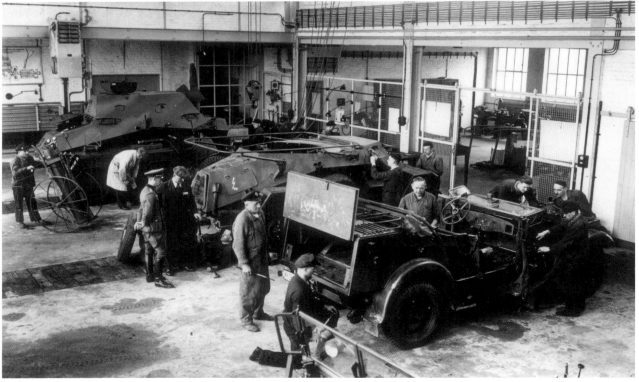

ABOVE: While doctrinally devoted to defense of the air space above formations, antiaircraft elements of both the *Luftwaffe* and the army increasingly saw themselves involved in ground combat as the war progressed. Theoretically an entire battalion was assigned or attached to a division to accomplish this role, although attrition and availability of weaponry often reduced the number of guns significantly. In this image, a bored *Luftwaffe* gun crew rolls through a German village aboard its Opel 1-ton truck, which is towing a *2cm FlaK 30*. The antiaircraft gun was designed in the early 1930s and started serial production in 1935. Although the weapon gradually gave way to the more advanced *FlaK 38*, which had a faster rate of fire and was less prone to jamming, the *FlaK 30* saw operational use until the end of the war.

FACING PAGE TOP: Tactical vehicles require an enormous amount of preventive maintenance to keep them running. In field conditions, repairs—both mechanical and those caused by battlefield damage—were the order of the day and maintenance personnel were the unsung heroes of all armored elements. In the prewar environment, maintenance, upgrade, and repair of a major nature often fell within the purview of civil service technicians and contract laborers. In these images, we see signals armored cars and a staff car under repair. In the background is an *Sd.Kfz. 263 (8-Rad)*, the mainstay of armored signals and armored reconnaissance battalions through the first half of the war. The large frame antenna has not been mounted, and its engine and rear deck armor have been removed. In the foreground is a light armored radio car, the *Sd.Kfz. 223*, which has had its machine-gun turret removed. It has a lightning bolt and the numeral *39* painted on its rear side, which might possibly indicate that these vehicles served with *Panzernachrichten-Abteilung 39* of the *3. Panzer-Division*.

FACING PAGE BOTTOM: In the second image, an additional vehicle, possibly the signals version of the *Sd.Kfz. 2*, can be seen as well. Given the large variety of vehicles seen here, this might be some sort of training facility for mechanics who specialized in communications vehicles. (MICHAEL H. PRUETT)

ABOVE: Prior to the start of hostilities in 1939 and, indeed, into the early war years, the *Panzerabwehrkanone 36* was Germany's main antitank weapon. The 37mm gun was already proving obsolescent in 1940 against French armor and turned out to be completely outclassed by the Soviets in 1941, when the T34 and the KV series of tanks began to be fielded against the Germans. It was replaced by guns of increasingly larger caliber and penetrating ability, starting with the 5cm *PaK 38* in mid-1940. This *PaK 36* is being towed by a *Kfz. 2.* (MICHAEL H. PRUETT)

FACING PAGE: Artillery supporting the armored force went through many iterations during the war, to include the introduction of self-propelled artillery, but the mainstays of the divisional artillery were the 10.5cm gun, the *leichte Feldhaubitze 18*, and later the 15cm howitzer, the *schwere Feldhaubitze 18*. The 10.5cm guns were generally found in the two artillery battalions of the prewar divisional artillery regiment, with a battalion of heavy guns designated to be attached to the divisional artillery in the event of mobilization. During the war, the heavy battalion was made an organic part of the divisional artillery. With the introduction of self-propelled artillery in 1943—the 10.5cm *Wespe* and the 15cm *Hummel*—the divisional artillery was supposed to receive at least one battery of each, but towed artillery remained a mainstay of even panzer divisions until the end of the war. In this image, a gun crew trains on a *schwere Feldhaubitze 18* in prewar exercises. Firing separately cased ammunition, the gun had a sustained rate of fire of four rounds a minute and could engage targets to a distance of 13,250 meters. Around 5,400 guns, including several upgrades, were produced. (MICHAEL H. PRUETT)

An *Sd.Kfz. 11* as seen at the German International Automotive Exposition of 1938 in Berlin. Although these prime movers were used to move a variety of equipment, they are most often associated with the artillery, especially the *leichte Feldhaubitze 18*. A prewar camouflage pattern has been applied to the sides and hood of the vehicle. In the second image, we see an 18-ton *Sd.Kfz. 9*, frequently referred to as a *Famo*, the heaviest prime mover half-track employed by the German Army during the war. It was used to tow the *schwere Feld-Haubitze 18*. (MICHAEL H. PRUETT)

CHAPTER 2

The Campaign in Poland (1939)

When Germany invaded Poland on September 1, 1939 (*Fall Weiß*, or "Case White"), the force ratio appeared approximately equal on paper. On the frontier with Poland, the *Wehrmacht* fielded 52 divisions and brigades with 1,500,000 men, and the Polish Army comprised 49 divisions and brigades with 1,300,000 men. However, these numbers are deceptive, as the German divisions included 15 armored and motorized divisions containing the majority of the approximately 3,600 armored vehicles in the German inventory. In contrast, the Poles fielded 11 cavalry brigades, which were of very limited use in modern warfare, and 2 mechanized brigades, with only about 850 armored vehicles, including 100 armored cars. In terms of artillery and aircraft, there was a similar disparity, with the German forces deploying 6,000 guns and 1,900 aircraft to the Poles' 4,000 guns and 900 aircraft.

The Germans' order of battle included five panzer divisions and four light divisions distributed among five field armies. The 1939 panzer division was a very well balanced combined-arms formation. In addition to its two panzer regiments, it included the following motorized formations: an infantry brigade consisting of two infantry regiments and a motorcycle infantry battalion, an artillery regiment with two medium artillery battalions (in theory, 36 *leichte Feldhaubitze 18*s of 10.5cm), a reconnaissance battalion, an antitank battalion, a combat engineer battalion, and a signals battalion. Also organic to the division were various support elements such as supply, maintenance, bakery, medical, ambulance, etc. Antiaircraft support was supplied by an attached *Luftwaffe* formation, generally of battalion size. In general, a heavy artillery battalion was also attached (later being assigned to the divisional artillery). Essentially, the division was a self-supporting entity capable of undertaking most required combat missions with its own assets. The light divisions, a kind of mechanized cavalry division, with their reduced numbers of main battle tanks, were not a success and soon converted into full panzer divisions. Most of the light divisions fielded only one battalion with 70 to 100 tanks. In some cases, these were predominantly Czech *Panzer 35(t)*s and *38(t)*s (*1.* and *4. leichte Division*).

Despite the superior number of tanks the Germans had, the composition of the force left much to be desired in terms of doctrinal suitability, with most of the force composed of light tanks that were on the verge of obsolescence, if not already obsolete. By way of example, let us look at the

1. Panzer-Division on September 1, 1939: *Panzer I*, 93 tanks; *Panzer II*, 122; *Panzer III*, 26; *Panzer IV*, 56. This amounted to a total of 297 tanks. The *1. Panzer-Division* was better equipped than the other armored divisions and was allocated more of the scarce *Panzer III*s and *IV*s. In 1939 only 206 of the *Panzer III* and 147 of the *Panzer IV* were produced. These two vehicles were intended to be the backbone of the panzer companies, although the *Panzer IV* was only initially intended to be a support tank inasmuch as it was armed with a 7.5cm main gun of only 24 calibers. The *Panzer III* and *IV* were well designed, reliable, combat capable, and, most importantly, able to be significantly upgraded.

In combat, most of the German tanks were more than a match for their Polish counterparts, both in terms of quantity and quality. The most numerous Polish tanks were the light TK and TKS tankettes of 2.5 tons, with 2 to 10mm of armor and armed with a single 7.92mm Hotchkiss machine gun. Nearly 600 of these vehicles were in service by September 1, 1940. Some of the TKSs were in the process of being rearmed with a 20mm NKM automatic cannon, capable of dealing with the lighter of the German tanks, but only about 24 were up-gunned by September. The best tank in Polish service was the 7TPjw, based on the British Vickers E, with about 90 of these tanks available. It had 5 to 17mm of armor, weighed 9.4 tons, and was armed with a 37mm Bofors gun that was superior in armor-penetrating capability to the 3.7cm of the *Panzer III*. The 7TPjw was the principal tank of the two mechanized brigades and a better combat vehicle than the majority of German tanks, but far too few were in service to affect the course of the campaign.

The remainder of tanks available to Polish forces were 100 obsolete French FT 17s dating from the First World War and 50 Renault R35 infantry tanks, of which only a handful saw combat. What armor was available was distributed to independent scout companies of infantry divisions, armored troops of cavalry brigades, and the mechanized brigades. Armor was considered subordinate to the infantry and cavalry and therefore not concentrated.

The other armored vehicles issued in significant numbers to the Germans were the armored cars equipping the reconnaissance and signals elements. Although there were a number of vehicles of generally good design—the four-wheeled *Sd.Kfz. 221*, *222*, and *223* and the eight-wheeled *Sd.Kfz. 231*, *232*, and *263* among them—the reconnaissance elements had to make do with overall shortfalls of equipment and a number of obsolescent or inadequate designs as well.

***

Germany's plan called for its five field armies to cut the Polish corridor separating East Prussia from the rest of Germany while simultaneously attacking to the south from East Prussia toward Warsaw and from the southwest from the German frontier to create a huge pincer movement designed to cut off and surround the majority of the Polish Army. The engagements along the national boundaries met with very determined resistance and no initial large-scale breakthrough took place along most of the front, although the armored units were quick to exploit any gaps in the defenses. The initial breakthrough had to be made by the infantry.

Once the initial breakthroughs occurred, the Poles continued to fight desperately and bravely, but they could not withstand the overwhelming German forces, particularly the armored formations that moved with unprecedented speed. With complete air superiority, the Germans completed their breakthrough by September 5, with the armored and motorized divisions sweeping all before them and encircling large numbers of Polish forces. By this stage the *Luftwaffe* was operating almost solely in a tactical manner, directly supporting the rampaging panzer and motorized divisions, which were advancing 24 kilometers a day in some cases. The Pozna Army, the last sizable intact Polish force defending Warsaw, was encircled and destroyed from September 9 to 17, with the Soviets advancing from the east the same day. A heavily bombed Warsaw capitulated on September 27, and a defeated Poland surrendered to the Germans and the Soviets at the beginning of October 1939.

The Germans had won a stunning victory, and the operations of the *Panzertruppe* exceeded even the most sanguine expectations. General Heinz

Guderian—known as the "founding father" of the panzer forces and commander of the *XIX. Armee-Korps (mot)*, consisting of the *3. Panzer-Division*, the *2. Infanterie-Division (mot),* and the *20. Infanterie-Division (mot)*—received a surprise visit from Adolf Hitler on September 5. When Hitler was shown a destroyed Polish artillery regiment, he had the following exchange with Guderian:

"'Our dive bombers did that?'

When I replied, 'No, our tanks!' he [Hitler] was plainly astonished."

Although vehicle and aircraft losses were high, the numbers of dead and wounded were surprisingly low, with some 13,000 killed and 30,000 wounded. This was certainly far lower than those suffered in the grinding attritional battles of World War I.

A *Panzer II* passes an *Sd.Kfz. 263* on an unimproved road in Poland. The *Sd.Kfz. 263* appears to have been christened with the name *Königgrätz*, in honor of the decisive battle of the Austro-Prussian War. The other marking on the left front slope of the communications vehicle remains unidentified.

ABOVE: This *Panzer II* appears to have become a "hangar queen" after battlefield damage or extensive mechanical problems made it impossible to be returned to the battlefield before the end of the campaign. Given the perennial shortage of armored vehicles within the inventories of German armored formations, "cannibalization" was often the only way to keep the remaining vehicles in the fleet running. The *Balkenkreuz* was in use during the campaign in Poland as a means of identifying German vehicles and avoiding friendly fire incidents. As the Germans discovered, however, it also made for a convenient aiming point for enemy gunners. As a result, it was discontinued after the campaign. The German numbering system for vehicles indicates that *Panzer II 145* was assigned to the 1st Company's 4th Platoon and was the 5th tank in the platoon. While vehicle numerals and *Balkenkreuze* were normally done in white during the campaign, this vehicle appears to have yellow numerals and a yellow *Balkenkreuz* outlined in white.

FACING PAGE TOP: *Sd.Kfz. 263*s return to Germany after the campaign in Poland is over. The heavy signals armored cars were possibly assigned to *Aufklärungs-Regiment 7 (mot)*, which was assigned to the *2. leichte Division*. After the campaign, the *2. leichte Division* was disbanded, with most of its elements going to form the *7. Panzer-Division*. The 1st Battalion of the regiment became the division's reconnaissance battalion, *Aufklärungs-Abteilung 7 (mot)*, and the 2nd Battalion became the motorcycle infantry battalion of the division, *Kradschützen-Bataillon 7*.

FACING PAGE BOTTOM: This *Panzer II*, possibly an *Ausführung B*, is parked next to a staff car from an artillery unit during a break in the campaign. Of interest is the bank of smoke dischargers on the rear of the vehicle. The dischargers were connected to the fighting compartment via cables and could be fired individually. These were used to mask retrograde movements of the tank in case it had to pull back under fire.

CHAPTER 3

The Campaign in the Low Countries and France (1940)

The Germans carefully evaluated the numerous lessons from the Polish campaign and were quick to act on them. In some instances, cooperation between armor and infantry had been poor, and more intensive training was initiated. The motorized infantry divisions were too large and cumbersome, so one infantry regiment was removed, usually reassigned to the newly forming panzer divisions. The light divisions had been less than successful in combat and were converted into panzer divisions, the 6th through the 9th. It was deemed urgent to equip the panzer regiments with the *Panzer III* and *IV* tanks; however, this proceeded slowly due to the limited capacity of industry. From January to April 1940 only 190 *Panzer III*s and less than 100 *Panzer IV*s were produced.

Therefore, as of May 10, 1940, of the approximately 3,500 tanks in total inventory, some 2,400 were still *Panzer I*s and *II*s, with 429 *Panzer III*s, 296 *Panzer IV*s, and 391 *Panzer 35(t)*s and *38(t)*s. There was also an urgent requirement to increase the armor of the *Panzer II*, as the 7.92mm *wz.35 UR*, the standard Polish antitank rifle, could penetrate its frontal armor at more than 100 yards. By May 1940 some 70 percent of the *Panzer II*s had been up-armored by welding additional 20mm plates to the hull, superstructure, and turret front. By now the *Panzer I* had been limited to scouting duties for the panzer regiments, although against infantry and soft-skinned vehicles it could lay down a deadly curtain of fire.

Looking at the *1. Panzer-Division* again, it had the following vehicles available in May 1940: *Panzer I*, 52; *Panzer II*, 98; *Panzer III*, 58; *Panzer IV*, 40; command tanks, 8; armored cars, 61.

Major problems with the panzer divisions that became evident during the Polish campaign were their lack of supporting infantry and the inability of truck-borne infantry to keep up with the tanks on the battlefield. Fortunately, a suitable vehicle was in production, the excellent *Sd.Kfz. 251* semi-tracked medium armored personnel carrier. This was a 9-ton vehicle capable of accommodating an infantry squad. The 8 to 14.5mm armor was capable of resisting small-arms fire, and the two mounted *MG34* machine guns could lay down suppressing fire. As was the case with almost all tactical vehicles, however, German industry was incapable of producing the numbers required and most panzer divisions only had a company of these vehicles within their motorized rifle regiments. This was a problem that was never satisfactorily solved. Even at the end of the war, it was a rare division that had a complete battalion outfitted with them.

***

At the start of the campaign, around 2,400 German tanks were issued to the 10 panzer divisions. They faced some 3,400 Allied tanks. It was not only in numbers that the Allies were superior but also in quality, with many of their tanks both better armed and armored. The four French armored divisions (*Divisions Cuirassées de Reserve*, or *DCR*) deployed 70 Renault *Char B1 bis* tanks, and 90 Hotchkiss H39s or Renault R35s with attached cavalry units comprising 40 Somua S35s. Armament was a 37mm main gun for the H39 and R35 and a 47mm main gun for the S35 and *B1 bis*, the latter of which was also armed with a 75mm cannon in the hull front. These tanks were virtually impervious to the main gun of the *Panzer III* and the standard *PaK 36* antitank gun. The main shortcomings of the French tanks were their relatively slow speeds and limited radius of action.

The British 1st Armoured Division was equipped with 140 Mark IV Cruiser tanks, which were reasonably well armored at 30mm and armed with a 2-pounder (40mm) main gun that had almost twice the effective range of the German 3.7cm main/antitank gun and superior penetrating power. The 4th and 7th Battalions' Royal Tank Regiments were equipped with 100 Infantry Tank Mark II Matildas. Like the Mark IV Cruiser, they were armed with a 2-pounder main gun. With 78mm of frontal armor, the Matilda was the most heavily armored tank in service at that time, but this was offset by a top speed of only 15mph.

The main problem for the Allies was not the vehicles but their deployment. Allied armor was not concentrated but scattered across the whole battlefront. The French allocated their vehicles to 4 armored, 3 mechanized, and 5 cavalry divisions as well as 33 tank battalions and 12 tank companies. Even the tanks within the armored divisions were often dispersed and not concentrated. In the case of the British Expeditionary Force, the tanks were spread among 8 cavalry regiments and 2 army tank battalions. The French Cavalry Group commander,

General Charles Delestraint, summed up the situation quite succinctly: "We had 3,000 tanks and so did the Germans. We used them in a thousand packs of three, the Germans in three packs of a thousand."

***

The four Allied field armies ponderously advanced to the Dyle Line in Belgium on May 10, 1940, in response to the attack of *Heeresgruppe B* (Field Army Group B), in expectation of a repeat of the Schlieffen Plan of World War I. This was exactly what the Germans had planned for, as it allowed *Heeresgruppe A* and its eight *Panzer* divisions to force their way through the supposedly tank-proof Ardennes and reach the Meuse River on May 12.

The breakthrough at Sedan and subsequent exploitation by the armored elements illustrated the capabilities of the panzer divisions. The *7. Panzer-Division*, commanded by Erwin Rommel, first crossed the Meuse at Dinant early on May 13. Later that day, Guderian's *Panzergruppe* (a corps equivalent) crossed at Sedan. The difficult crossings were accomplished by the reconnaissance forces, tanks, infantry, and artillery all working in concert with continuous tactical air support provided by the *Luftwaffe*. One of the keys to this success was the superb command and control procedures, with a continuous flow of radio traffic between the front-line units, rear headquarters, and support units. Decisions were made according to the immediate situation by division and corps commanders who led from the front. On the contrary, the Allied command system was both inefficient and sluggish, often relying on preplanned responses to situations that were no longer current.

The subsequent breakthrough was spearheaded by the reconnaissance troops with their motorcycles and armored cars, closely followed by the panzer elements accompanying infantry and artillery towed by half-tracks. The panzers exploded into the open, largely undefended countryside and headed straight for the coast in order to cut off the Allied field armies in the north. Apart from some minor delays imposed by nervous commanders at higher headquarters, the channel was reached on May 20. There were some minor counterattacks by the French at Laon from May 17 to 19 and the British at Arras on

May 21, but the heavy tanks were countered by field artillery and *Luftwaffe* 88mm antiaircraft guns used in the antiaircraft role. In general, the German advance was largely unimpeded.

During the second half of the campaign, there was some heavy fighting in the south against Weygand's "hedgehog defense"; however, the armored forces of generals Kleist and Guderian broke through French defense lines. With the assistance of the *Luftwaffe*, which destroyed concentrations of French artillery, the German armor bypassed centers of resistance and encircled the defending forces. With the majority of French armor and troops either destroyed or captured, the end was inevitable. On June 22 the French signed an armistice that took effect on June 25.

***

The Germans had won one of the most stunning military victories in history. From 1914 to 1918, all sides of the conflict had suffered millions of dead and wounded. The 1940 campaign had cost the German Army 27,000 killed, 111,000 wounded, and 13,400 missing. The conquest of France and the Low Countries had taken a scant six weeks.

Despite the success, there were many lessons to be learned from the campaign. In particular, there was an urgent need to replace the remaining *Panzer Is* and *IIs*, with the former now totally unsuited for combat and the latter suitable only for reconnaissance. The *Panzer III* urgently needed rearming with a heavier weapon. Its main gun had proven totally ineffective against the majority of French and British tanks. This was accomplished by upgrading to the larger and longer caliber *5cm KwK L/42* in the latter production run of the *Ausführung F* and the *Ausführung G*. Armor was increased to 30mm at the hull rear. On the *Ausführung H*, produced from October 1940 to April 1941, armor was increased by the addition of 30mm plates at the front and rear. Somewhat inexplicably, the *Panzer III* was not up-gunned with the far more effective *5cm KwK L/60* used in the newly introduced *PaK 38* antitank gun, contrary to Hitler's express order. This was to prove a serious shortcoming for this vehicle when the Soviet Union was invaded.

On the *Panzer IV, Ausführung E*, which was produced from September 1940 to April 1941, the armor at the upper front of the hull was increased by the addition of 30mm plate. Additional plates of 20mm thickness were added at the rear. The lower hull remained at 50mm. No change was made to the armament of this version of the tank.

In order to counter heavier tanks, the chassis of the *Panzer I* was used to mount the effective Czech *4.7cm PaK(t) L/43.4*. From March 1940 to February 1941, 202 *Panzer I, Ausführung Bs* were converted. This was the first of many conversions using an obsolete chassis to mount heavier weapons than originally carried, thereby giving greater mobility to the antitank units.

A less successful conversion was the attempt to mount a *15cm sIG 33* infantry howitzer on the chassis of a *Panzer I, Ausführung B*, of which 38 were converted in February 1940. Equipping heavy infantry gun companies (701 to 706), they were allocated to six panzer divisions for the invasion of Belgium and France. This vehicle was top-heavy and unstable, and the chassis was overloaded. Subsequent versions on other chassis were much better designed. Nonetheless, this marked one of the first steps to create self-propelled artillery that was capable of keeping pace with the other armored elements.

A far more successful vehicle was the *Sturmgeschütz III, Ausführung A* assault gun, which used the hull of the *Panzer III, Ausführung F*, with a low-profile superstructure mounting a limited-traverse *7.5cm StuK 37 L/24*. The *StuG III* was intended as a direct-fire infantry support vehicle. Thirty were issued to *Sturmartillerie* batteries 640, 659, 660, and 665 and went into action in France, where their combat performance was highly praised by the infantry elements they supported. The *StuG III* was to become one of the most important armored vehicles of the war, even though the assault-gun elements were technically part of the artillery branch.

FACING PAGE TOP: Scenes like this are typically found in German soldier albums of the period: long columns of German forces advancing without incident through border defenses and fortifications. (MICHAEL H. PRUETT)

FACING PAGE BOTTOM: A traffic jam of armored elements along an unimproved dirt road in France. Thanks to mild weather, expansive fields and farmlands, and an extended road network, tanks could usually avoid scenes such as this. Based on vehicle positioning, these elements are possibly staging for the onset of a new day of operations. Given the limited space within armored vehicles, personal items and "spoils of war" were often stored on the outside, as evidenced by the rear view of the *Panzerbefehlswagen III* on the right. (MICHAEL H. PRUETT)

BELOW: At this commanders' conference, an armor officer, most likely *Hauptmann* Adelbert Schulz, discusses operations with an unidentified *Oberstleutnant*, most likely the battalion or regimental commander of the element he is supporting. Schulz, who was the commander of the *I./Panzer-Regiment 25* of the *7. Panzer-Division*, later received the Knight's Cross for his actions during this campaign. By the time he was killed in action in January 1944, he was the commander of the same division and the recipient of the Knight's Cross with Oak Leaves, Swords and Diamonds.

    The swastika flag on top of the staff car is an aerial recognition panel intended to reduce incidents of friendly fire by the *Luftwaffe*. (MICHAEL H. PRUETT)

ABOVE: This *Panzer II* from the *7. Panzer-Division* was upended by either mines or closely impacting artillery shells. Given the wide-open area, the latter is most likely the cause, since mines are generally emplaced to cover obstacles or likely avenues of approach during fast-moving operations, when time is of the essence for the defender.

FACING PAGE: Several images of the *15cm sIG 33 (Sf) auf Panzerkampfwagen I, Ausführung B*, during the campaign in the West. Also referred to as the *Sturmpanzer I "Bison,"* this was the first attempt by the Germans to introduce a form of self-propelled artillery to the battlefield. A total of 38 of the vehicles were produced by the firm of Alkett by February 1940 and were assigned to six separate heavy infantry gun companies *(schwere Infanteriegeschütz-Kompanien)*, all of which were further attached to panzer divisions. Slow and unwieldy, the guns were nonetheless a welcome addition to the battlefield for the motorized infantry elements they supported. Although quickly phased out of service, some were still reported as being operational on front lines until 1943. The last image is of a *Bison* that was probably assigned to *schwere Infanteriegeschütz-Kompanie 705 (mot)*, which was attached to the *7. Panzer-Division*. (FIRST IMAGE: MICHAEL H. PRUETT)

FACING PAGE TOP: Tanks of the *7. Panzer-Division—Panzer II*s and *Panzer 38(t)*s of either *Panzer-Regiment 25* or *Panzer-Abteilung 66*—assemble for continued operations in France, while an *Sd.Kfz. 247, Ausführung B*, command and control vehicle, most likely from the divisional reconnaissance battalion *Aufklärungs-Abteilung 37 (mot)*, observes in the foreground. Only 58 of the lightly armored staff vehicles were produced, with some reportedly seeing service until war's end.

FACING PAGE BOTTOM: In the second image, possibly taken from the same general area, vehicles of the reconnaissance battalion—a mix of *Sd.Kfz. 221, 222*, and *223* armored cars—also stage, while smoke rises in the background.

BELOW: *Panzer I*s and *II*s of the *VI./Panzer-Regiment 25* appear to be taking an operational pause along an unimproved road in rural France. The tremendous distances covered during the campaign took their toll of wear and tear on the tracked vehicles. Minor track repairs could be done by vehicle crews with onboard equipment, but the *Panzer II* in the middle appears to have additional issues, since its weapons have also been removed.

ABOVE: Seen during the French campaign, a *4.7cm PaK(t) (Sf) auf Panzerkampfwagen I, Ausführung B*, is inspected by a general officer of mountain troops. His general-officer rank is indicated in several other photographs in this series, and his branch of service is indicated by his mountain cap with metal *Edelweiß* cap badge. The *Panzerjäger I*, as the vehicle was commonly known, was the first German self-propelled antitank gun to see service in World War II. It mounted a 4.7cm antitank gun of Czech origin on a modified *Panzer I* chassis. In all, some 202 of the vehicles were delivered for front-line service in France, North Africa, the Balkans, and the opening stages of the war against the Soviet Union, where they were assigned to separate antitank companies. Like subsequent designs based on the *Panzer II* chassis, the vehicles relied on mobility and stealth to seek out and destroy their targets, since the armor plating provided was only adequate against small-arms fire. (MICHAEL H. PRUETT)

FACING PAGE TOP: An *Sd.Kfz. 232 (8-Rad)* from an unidentified reconnaissance element crosses a temporary bridge, most likely constructed by combat engineers. In the absence of amphibious vehicles, bridges and fords provided the only crossing points for the rapid advance of motorized and armored forces. Divisional engineers were capable of constructing temporary bridging over short spans, but they generally had to resort to more conventional bridge-building techniques for larger bodies of water. In general, corps and higher-level engineering assets started building conventional bridges once the combat elements had moved forward, so that divisional engineers could retrieve and then reuse their organic bridging assets for future obstacles. The heavy armored car seen here was mostly likely in a rear area, since the crew has put the rain-resistant tarpaulin on the turret.

FACING PAGE BOTTOM: This *Panzer IV, Ausführung D*, most likely from *Panzer-Regiment 5* of the *3. Panzer-Division*, crosses another engineer bridge in a rear area. Most of the crew ride outside the vehicle and the turret hatches are open in an effort to beat the heat of summertime France.

LEFT: The turret of this *Sd.Kfz. 232 (8-Rad)* has been penetrated by a smaller-caliber antitank weapon. German armored cars were generally only capable of withstanding small-arms fire, which provided crews with a major incentive to adhere to the doctrinal dictum of "see and not be seen."

BELOW: This *Sd.Kfz. 251/1 (Wurfrahmen 40)* was a specially fitted half-track for use by German armored combat engineer battalions of the panzer divisions, the *Panzer-Pionier-Bataillon.* Delivery to the troops began in March 1941. The *Sd.Kfz. 251/1* had six side-mounted brackets for firing either 28, 30, or 32cm rockets, which were either high-explosive (30) or incendiary (28 and 32). An area-fire weapon, it made up for lack of accuracy by sheer volume of explosive power in a small area. The 30cm version was not introduced until 1943. The rockets were also fitted on other vehicles, notably captured stocks of the French Renault *UE Chenillette*, a light-tracked armored carrier, and the Hotchkiss H35, a light tank.

The same *Panzer IV, Ausführung D*, seen crossing the engineer bridge previously, are now being prepared for the rail trip home. Once the campaign was over, almost all of the wheeled and armored tactical assets of the divisions were transported by rail to avoid additional wear and tear on the vehicles. The *Panzer IV* was still considered a "heavy" tank by the Germans at this time and was only available in limited numbers within the panzer regiments (usually only one company per battalion). Of interest in this photograph is the "piggybacking" of the *Panzer I* from the same company on the railcar. In all, less than 500 *Panzer IV, Ausführung Ds* were produced.

ABOVE: *Panzer I*s and *Panzer II*s of the headquarters section of the *II./Panzer-Regiment 5* are lined up in a small French village at the end of the campaign. The regiment was later reassigned from the *3. Panzer-Division* to the newly formed *5. leichte Division* in February 1941, where it served with distinction in North Africa. After weeks of hard campaigning, personal items and stores found their way onto the rear decks of the vehicles due to the cramped quarters within the fighting compartments. The names seen on the backs of the turrets are those of fallen comrades. In the case of "Richard Schwandt" on *Panzer II 007*, he was a *Leutnant der Reserve*.

RIGHT: Memorials were also painted at other locations on vehicles, such as this more elaborate one to *Obergefreiter* Willi Schlatholt on the vision plate of a *Panzer II*. In addition to his rank and name, the date and location of his death are indicated.

TOP: Formerly in the service of the French Army, a Laffly is now employed by members of the maintenance section of the *1./ Aufklärungs-Abteilung (mot) 3* of the *3. Panzer-Division* to tow a disabled *Sd.Kfz. 232 (6-Rad)* from Lyon to Berlin, a distance of 1,500 kilometers. A crudely painted *WH* (*Wehrmacht*) appears on the front of the vehicle in lieu of a license plate. (MICHAEL H. PRUETT)

BOTTOM: In the second image, the Laffly appears to have dropped off its cargo, while one of the soldiers pays a visit to friends or family. His troop would later be reassigned to the *1. (Pz.Späh)/Aufklärungs-Abteilung (mot) 160* of the *60. Infanterie-Division* and was destroyed in Stalingrad. (MICHAEL H. PRUETT)

ABOVE: Reconnaissance elements staged somewhere in France, most likely in anticipation of being shipped home after the campaign. On view are *Sd.Kfz. 221, 223*, and *232 (6-Rad)* armored cars, as well as a host of motorcycles and soft-skin vehicles. Portions of the two-tone camouflage pattern of the time can be seen clearly on the *Sd.Kfz. 221* in the foreground.

FACING PAGE TOP: After the fall of France, large numbers of French vehicles were impressed into service by the German military forces. In this photograph, two soldiers of a field bakery proudly pose beside their Renault AGK truck. (MICHAEL H. PRUETT)

FACING PAGE BOTTOM: In the second instance, three Renault *UE Chenillette* light-tracked carriers have been taken over by new owners. (MICHAEL H. PRUETT)

CHAPTER 4

The Campaign in the Balkans (1941)

Although the Balkan region of Europe was not initially on Hitler's radar screen, the military misadventures of his ally, Mussolini's Italy, forced his hand. Italy invaded Greece in late October 1940. Its offensive soon stalled, the Greeks launched a counteroffensive, and Great Britain began sending forces and support. Partly to aid his struggling ally and partly to counter a perceived threat to Romanian oil fields, Hitler first sent forces to Romania and Bulgaria and then had plans drawn up to invade Greece. The situation was further complicated by a coup d'état in Yugoslavia on March 27, 1941, prompting Hitler to include that country in his invasion plans.

The campaign was launched on April 6, 1941, with Yugoslavia falling by April 17 and mainland Greece by April 30. On May 20 airborne forces stormed the island of Crete, which fell by June 1 with the surrender of remaining forces on the island. By the end of the fighting, Italy, Albania, Hungary, and Bulgaria had also joined the fray on the Axis side, in an effort to expand their power base in the region.

German forces essentially used the same maneuver warfare concepts against the Yugoslavians and the Greeks as had been used against France the previous year. They were aided and abetted by the almost complete dissolution of those forces, once initial defensive lines were breached. The reputation of the Germans preceded them and contributed to the general lack of will to fight. The exception, of course, was the British forces deployed there, but there were too few to make a decisive difference (approximately 60,000 in theater).

Historians continue to debate the effect the operational "detour" had on the invasion of the Soviet Union that was to follow that summer, since it delayed the German offensive by several months.

FACING PAGE TOP: During the invasion of Serbia, *Panzer-Regiment 15* of the *11. Panzer-Division* encountered a steel beam planted as a roadblock. A *Panzer II* has been called upon to act as a "bulldozer" and dislodge it. The tactical sign for the *11. Panzer-Division*—a yellow circle with a vertical line running through its center—can be seen in the center portion of the front upper hull of the tank. Obstacles like this need to be covered by fire to be effective. In this case, it merely served as a "speed bump" for the advance. (MICHAEL H. PRUETT)

FACING PAGE BOTTOM: The main reason why armored operations are not considered suitable for mountainous terrain can clearly be seen in this image. With much of the theater of operations covered by steep mountains and an underdeveloped road network, German armor's main role was for shock value against poorly trained and fielded armies. Forward progress was easily slowed by unimproved roadways and steep embankments; it could be completely stopped for extensive periods by a few cleverly emplaced obstacles. That said, German motorcycle forces achieved impressive results during the campaign, primarily by using their speed as a weapon.

ABOVE: Elements of a heavy artillery battalion move over a cobblestone bridge somewhere in an urban area in Serbia; in immediate view is a limbered *schwere Feldhaubitze 18* and its prime mover, an *Sd.Kfz. 7* half-track. The guns and prime movers appear to have had their fair share of use, as evidenced by their mud-splattered appearance.

ABOVE: This *sFH 18* has suffered a barrel burst, usually caused by wear and erosion to the barrel over time. Normally, barrels were replaced well before their scheduled "gun tube life" was reached, but the necessities of combat sometimes dictated the continued firing of pieces, even when it became a safety concern. Needless to say, such premature explosions could be deadly to the crew.

FACING PAGE TOP: German gun crews use captured ex-Czechoslovak 14.91cm howitzers, the *hrubá houfnice vzor 37*, in the mountainous terrain of the Balkans. In German service, it was redesignated as the *15cm schwere Feldhaubitze 37(t)*.

FACING PAGE BOTTPM: An *Sd.Kfz. 252* of *Sturmgeschütz-Abteilung 184* moves through a Yugoslavian town, where it is greeted by civilians in native garb. Due to ethnic strife, the Germans were considered "liberators" in certain sections of the country. The *Sd.Kfz. 252* was an ammunition carrier based on the chassis of the *Sd.Kfz. 250* and issued to assault gun batteries. More than 400 were manufactured from January to December 1941, before it was eventually replaced by the *Sd.Kfz. 250/6*. The crew member seen in the image wears the field-gray version of the special-purpose uniform for armored vehicle crews.

CHAPTER 5

The Campaign against the Soviet Union (1941)

The campaign in the East was so vast in scale, both in terms of territory encompassed—half of Europe—and the millions of troops engaged, that even the briefest description of the whole campaign would far exceed the scope of this book. Accordingly, this summary concentrates mainly on the use of armor and some technical details on both the composition of armored forces and on the armored vehicles employed.

On June 22, 1941, German forces staged in the East totaled 3,050,000 men in 207 divisions (13 motorized) and 3 brigades; 625,000 horses; 600,000 motor vehicles (including armored cars); and 3,350 armored fighting vehicles (excluding armored cars) in 17 panzer divisions. The *Luftwaffe* fielded almost 4,000 aircraft of all types, including liaison and transport, of which just over 3,000 were operational. It was the panzer divisions primarily allocated to Army Groups Center and South that were the spearhead of Operation Barbarossa, the invasion of the Soviet Union.

Facing the Germans and their allies were 3,000,000 Soviet troops on the front line with another 1,000,000 in reserve. In terms of armor, the Germans faced some 22,500 tanks and almost 5,000 armored cars, more than twice Guderian's prewar estimate of 10,000, which was considered a substantial exaggeration at the time. Impressive though these figures were, they concealed the considerable weaknesses of a badly led, inadequately trained, and poorly maintained tank force. Among the most numerous tanks were 11,000 T26s and 6,000 BT fast tanks. Only 970 of the vehicles were the revolutionary T34 medium tank. In addition, there were 500 of the heavy KV series. Both of the aforementioned tanks, however, were superior to anything the Germans fielded at the time.

The panzer divisions were attached to four panzer groups, which were field army equivalents, and concentrated in narrow sectors. They sliced through the Soviet border defenses in the initial onslaught, trapping hundreds of thousands of troops and destroying thousands of artillery pieces and tanks. The Soviet command structure on all levels was initially thrown into chaos, due to the disruption caused by the rapid German advance of more than 30 kilometers a day. The German high command was well aware of the need to destroy the Soviet armies west of the Dnieper River; however, the panzer forces were numerically inadequate for maintaining such an advance and also containing the vast number of surrounded Soviet forces. It has been argued, with some justification, that the effort required to reduce these pockets, particularly the one at Smolensk from July 10 to August 4, fatally disrupted the German timetable, overly optimistic as it was.

By early July the German high command considered victory close at hand. In less than three weeks, the Soviets had lost approximately 750,000 troops, nearly 12,000 tanks, some 4,000 aircraft, and 10,000 field pieces. Conversely, there were nearly 135,000 German casualties in the same period. Although the tank losses were relatively light at 118, panzer division strength was declining rapidly, with as many as 50 percent of the tank strength out of service at any given time due to maintenance issues, primarily caused by the primitive Russian roads. By August, there was no sign of a Soviet collapse. Despite the horrendous casualties, the number of Soviet divisions had actually increased to 212 by mid-July, although only about 90 were anywhere near full strength. The Germans had initially estimated a total of 200 Soviet divisions capable of combat operations, but by August the number had risen to no less than 360.

The initial tank battles were the largest of the entire war, with thousands of Soviet tanks attempting to stop the advance of the German armored groups. Even in these early engagements, the Germans were encountering the T34 and KV tanks, much to their shock and dismay. The T34 was far superior to the main German battle tank, the *Panzer III*. Although the frontal armor was about the same, it was sloped on the T34, which gave it superior protection. In addition, it mounted a high-velocity and heavier-caliber gun and its tracks were wider, giving superior cross-country mobility. Its lightweight diesel engine was also more robust and powerful than its German counterpart.

In these early engagements, victory was enabled thanks to superior German command and control. It was also assisted by the use of 105mm and 150mm field guns from divisional artillery firing over open sights. *Luftwaffe* ground support from the air and the employment of the 88mm *FlaK 18* and *36* on the ground saved the day for the Germans on many occasions.

In the case of the KV, it was a slower, heavier tank with a lower-velocity gun but more heavily armored. It was impervious to all German antitank guns, including the recently introduced 50mm *PaK 38* that could at least destroy the T34 at medium combat ranges (500 meters).

These new tanks would not be encountered in large numbers until the Soviet counteroffensive in December. Both types were not without their faults. They suffered from poor optics, limiting their ability to engage German tanks. In fact, when buttoned up, both vehicles were nearly blind. The T34 also had a very unreliable transmission. From a command and control perspective, only a small number of tanks had radios, severely limiting their coordination in combat. The major fault with regard to the T34 was its two-man turret; the tank commander also had to serve as loader, severely limiting his ability to lead the vehicle in combat.

***

Unlike the French campaign, where there was a clear strategic objective to drive to the English Channel and isolate the French and British armies in Belgium, the field army groups were sent in three directions with no overall strategic goal other than eliminating Soviet forces. The drive on Moscow was delayed by more than a month, when the momentum of the advance was stopped by the necessity of diverting forces to contain and eliminate huge pockets of Soviet forces. At Kiev, four Soviet field armies and parts of a fifth—some 43 divisions—were trapped. The Germans claimed 652,000 prisoners and the Soviets themselves admitted to 616,000 casualties. However, valuable time was lost, allowing the Soviet forces to recuperate with astonishing rapidity. On the German side, casualties continued to mount, and by late August the Eastern Front was short 200,000 troops and most panzer divisions were down to 20 to 30 percent of their initial tank strength.

After a delay of a month, a result mainly of conflicting priorities, the drive on Moscow—Operation *Taifun* (Typhoon)—continued with three panzer groups, consisting of eight motorized corps, as the spearhead. The motorized corps had been reinforced by 300 replacement tanks and the *2. Panzer-Division* and the *5. Panzer-Division* (with 400 tanks between them). In total, the German forces consisted of 1,930,000 troops, 1,500 tanks, and 14,000 field pieces pitted against an estimated 54 Soviet divisions. As usual, the Germans badly underestimated the Soviet forces, which consisted of 83 rifle divisions, 13 tank brigades (with 850 tanks, mostly light BT-series and T26s), and 1,250,000 men. Those were far stronger forces than had been available a month earlier.

Guderian's *Panzergruppe 2*, with its 405 tanks, started the offensive on September 30, smashing through the Bryansk Front. Two days later, Hoth's and Hoepner's *Panzergruppen* advanced rapidly, establishing bridgeheads over the Dnieper, destroying two Soviet field armies, and encircling three more in the process. The Vyazma and Bryansk pockets collapsed on October 14 and 18, with more than 1,000,000 Soviet troops killed, wounded, or taken prisoner. However, as had occurred previously, 7 of the 14 panzer divisions were required to contain and eliminate the pockets, thereby drastically reducing offensive capabilities.

In early October the autumn rains commenced—the start of the soon-to-be-dreaded *Rasputitsa* mud season—turning the already terrible roads into almost impassable quagmires that were difficult to negotiate even by tracked vehicles. The already inadequate German motor transport, consisting of far too many types, including a significant number of captured vehicles, could not cope with the conditions and supplies to the attacking divisions were severely curtailed, with less than half of the required tonnage being delivered.

Operation Typhoon ground on against increasing Soviet resistance and increasingly unfavorable weather until the end of October. Another operation was launched on November 15, and by the end of the month, reconnaissance units were in the outer suburbs of Moscow. By early December the drive to Moscow was finally halted in the face of freezing weather, determined Soviet resistance, and lack of reinforcements, with *Panzergruppe 3* down to a mere 77 tanks. The *Wehrmacht* had not prepared for a Russian winter: Lubricants froze, engines would not start, guns would not fire, winter uniforms were essentially unavailable, and no significant reinforcements were forthcoming.

It was at this moment that the Soviets launched a counterattack with 52 rifle divisions, 3 tank divisions, and 5 tank brigades, a total of 640,000 men and 600 tanks, the majority of them T34s. The counteroffensive was devastating, with *Heeresgruppe Mitte* pushed back along its entire front. However, there was no large-scale breakthrough and the German forces did not collapse, with Hitler ordering his forces to hold in place rather than conducting an elastic defense that they were not capable of executing. The remaining tanks were the focal point of the German "hedgehog" defenses of villages and towns that offered both cover and protection from the brutal Russian winter.

The Soviet counteroffensive was far too ambitious in scope, seeking to surround and destroy Army Group Center. Instead of reinforcing Zhukov, the Soviet commander in chief, which could have led to a breakthrough, attacking forces were scattered all along the front, which, in the end, achieved little except for the creation of two dangerous salients. Both sides suffered significant casualties: some 400,000 for the Germans and almost 2,000,000 for the Soviets. The spring rains halted both Soviet offensive operations and German counterattacks, with both sides regrouping for the summer offensives.

The result of the appearance of the T34 and KV tanks that totally outclassed their German counterparts led to a concerted effort to up-gun the existing *Panzer III*s and *IV*s. The *Panzer III* began to mount a 50mm main gun of 60 calibers, while the *Panzer IV* saw its main gun being lengthened—first to 43 and then to 48 calibers—thus dramatically increasing its anti-armor capabilities. Both of these tanks were issued to panzer divisions in early 1942. As a result, the *Panzer IV* could now engage the T34s and KVs at all combat ranges.

It was also decided to employ the existing chassis of obsolete tanks to mount heavier guns capable of defeating the T34 and KV. In this, the Germans were extremely successful with the *Marder I* and *III* series of tank hunters based on the chassis of the *Panzer II* (777 produced) and the *Panzer 38(t)* (780 produced or converted from existing chassis). These mounted either the 76mm Soviet gun, the *PaK 36(r)*, re-chambered for German ammunition, or the 75mm *PaK 40*. They were stopgap vehicles, open-topped and lightly armored and not intended for direct combat against tanks, although this often occurred in the heat of battle. Nonetheless, when employed properly, they were effective against Soviet armor.

Originally intended as an infantry support vehicle, a very effective tank-killer was the *Sturmgeschütz III*. The *Ausführung F* and *Ausführung G* were produced from March 1942 onwards and adapted to mount the powerful 75mm *StuK 40*. Relatively well protected with 80mm of front hull armor, they were low and difficult to spot. In addition, they were very maneuverable, thus allowing the *StuG III* to be a formidable opponent of Soviet armor until the last days of the war. They were issued not only to separate assault gun battalions but also to panzer and *Panzergrenadier* divisions, due to the chronic shortfall in the production of tanks. More than 8,400 of the *StuG III* mounting the long 75mm main gun were produced.

These stopgap measures were very effective, and from 1942 onwards the Germans and Soviets were involved in a hectic gun/armor race that saw some impressive and innovative armored vehicles produced. Until the middle of 1944, the Germans actually prevailed, at least in terms of quality if not quantity, as the Soviets, almost inexplicably, lost their early commanding lead.

FACING PAGE TOP: A scene reminiscent of the opening stages of the campaign against the Soviet Union: Rapidly advancing forces seize prized objects such as intact bridges over water obstacles which, in turn, facilitate the continuation of the advance. In this instance, the tank commander of a *Panzer II* from *Panzer-Abteilung (Fl) 101* keeps a watchful eye on ground approaches to the bridge, while *Luftwaffe* gunners manning a 2cm *FlaK 38* guard the skies. The rear deck of the *Panzer II* is practically overflowing with personal items, stores, extra ammunition, and other items needed for extended campaigning. In December 1941 this battalion, which was a general headquarters flamethrower element, was consolidated with the newly forming *Panzer-Regiment 24* of the *24. Panzer-Division*.

FACING PAGE BOTTOM: In the next image, reconnaissance assets pass a shot-down and burned-out Soviet *Rata* fighter.

TOP: *Major* Müller, the commander of *Minenräum-Abteilung 1*, the very first German remote (radio) controlled formation, talks to a local farmer during exercises conducted by the battalion shortly before its deployment to the East in 1941. Equipped with Borgward BI and BII remotely piloted mine-clearing vehicles, the mission of the battalion was to clear lanes through enemy minefields. The battalion was employed with mixed success in the summer of 1941, before it was reorganized and redesignated as *Panzer-Abteilung 300*.

BOTTOM: A heavy armored car section, consisting of an *Sd.Kfz. 231 (8-Rad)* and an *Sd.Kfz. 232 (8-Rad)*, moves across an open area in a small Soviet town. When conducting operations, the *Sd.Kfz. 231* usually took the lead and performed most of the actual scouting, while the *Sd.Kfz. 232* would linger more to the rear and relay information back to higher headquarters. In this manner, communications could be maintained with headquarters, even if the lead vehicle happened to become disabled or knocked out.

These armored cars, an *Sd.Kfz. 223* and an *Sd.Kfz. 232 (8-Rad)*, both attributed to *Aufklärungs-Abteilung 5 (mot)*, have had their bed-frame antennas removed, possibly to facilitate some maintenance work. The angular device on the front of the *Sd.Kfz. 232 (8-Rad)* was referred to as a *Zerschellerplatte*—literally, shattering plate—which was designed to shatter or deflect small-caliber rounds before impacting the hull. The space behind the stand-off armor was often also used by crews to store personal items. Although the outbuilding and the uniforms would point to a prewar or early war image, the "open" *Balkenkreuz* and the large block *G* on the *Sd.Kfz. 232 (8-Rad)* indicate the Soviet Union and attachment of the division to *Panzergruppe G* (GUDERIAN).

This *Sd.Kfz. 222* of the *1. (Panzerspäh)/ Aufklärungs-Abteilung 160* of the *60. Infanterie-Division (mot)* was photographed in Russia during inclement weather. Of interest is the seldom-seen dark gray canvas protection cover for the armament and turret. A small *NSDAP* pennant hangs from the fender guide pole. The vehicle commander wears the *Krad-mantel* (protective coat for motorcyclists), an item that was frequently obtained and worn by armored vehicle crews. Also of interest is the rope wrapped around the front bumper, which was used to help tow vehicles or extricate them when bogged down in soft terrain. (MICHAEL H. PRUETT)

FACING PAGE TOP: In these images, a rare German flamethrower variant can be seen, the *Flammwagen auf Panzerkampfwagen B-2(f)*. It is being towed through the town of Lemberg (present-day Lviv in Ukraine) after some mechanical problem. The original photograph is dated July 4, 1941. (MICHAEL H. PRUETT)

FACING PAGE BOTTOM: In the second image, the prime mover for the tank, an 18-ton *Famo* half-track, is visible. A white vehicle number, *223*, appears on the rear of the turret. This vehicle is believed to have been assigned to *Panzer-Abteilung (F) 102*, which had two flamethrower companies. Each company had 12 of the modified *Char B1 bis* tanks and 3 tanks that retained their original 75mm main-gun armament. By the end of July the battalion was disbanded, with its remaining assets being distributed among several other special-purpose tank battalions that fought in the East, the West, and the Balkans. (MICHAEL H. PRUETT)

ABOVE: The headquarters section of a motorcycle infantry battalion moves through difficult terrain. Even in the rather ideal campaigning conditions of summer, a cloudburst could transform most unimproved Soviet roads into impassable quagmires. The large *G* seen on several of the vehicles stands for *Panzergruppe Guderian*. The *Sd.Kfz. 251* seen coming down the slope is one of the command and control versions of the vehicle, an early *Sd.Kfz. 251/3*.

FACING PAGE TOP: German soldier albums from the first year of the war in the East are filled with images of knocked-out, destroyed, abandoned, and/or captured Soviet equipment. In the first image, we see a Voroshilovets tractor, which served as a prime mover for artillery pieces, mostly the 152 and 203mm howitzers, before being phased out of service in 1942.

FACING PAGE BOTTOM: Serving with a German artillery unit on the Eastern Front is an ex-British Scammell R100 artillery tractor. A "chain" of captured Russian field guns are in tow. They appear to be 76.2mm *Pushka obr. 1902/30 g L/30* and *L/40L* field guns. Some interesting markings are painted on this vehicle, such as crossed cannons on the cab and the numbers *3/19* (ex-British) stenciled on both the fender and the door. A large white swastika has also been painted on the driver's door, undoubtedly to help avoid friendly fire incidents.

FACING PAGE TOP: A knocked-out or abandoned early version of the T34 elicits curiosity from the German soldiers passing it in their horse-drawn vehicle. Armed with a long-barreled 76mm main gun, the tank was vastly superior to anything the Germans fielded at the time and caused considerable psychological shock to the advancing German forces when it was first encountered in the summer of 1941. The only weapons that could directly defeat it at normal battlefield ranges were the 88mm *FlaK* and divisional artillery firing over open sights. Otherwise, a great deal of luck or steely nerves was generally required to knock it out in tank-on-tank combat. Fortunately for the Germans, the T34s were generally poorly employed, with only company commanders having radios, thus making it easier to counter them.

FACING PAGE BOTTOM: The Germans immediately evacuated many of the intact T34s they encountered in the summer of 1941 for technical evaluation. If a vehicle could be made combat-ready again, it was often impressed into German service, albeit oftentimes with some modifications by the Germans, particularly with regard to signals equipment. In this image, a T34/76 with steel-rimmed roadwheels has been loaded onto a tank transporter trailer, the *Sonder-Anhänger 116,* and towed by an 18-ton *Famo* half-track for its journey to the rear.

ABOVE: A German armored column passes an artillery observation vehicle along an unimproved road in the northern Soviet Union. Although the unit was not identified in this image, the terrain and the presence of a *Panzer 35(t)* on the viewer's far right are clues linking the image to *Panzer-Regiment 11* of the *6. Panzer-Division*, the only major formation that still used the outmoded vehicles in the Soviet Union and also participated in the drive on Leningrad.

ABOVE AND FACING PAGE: As the campaign continued into the fall, the weather started turning correspondingly colder. These motorcycle infantry are attributed to *Kradschützen-Bataillon 1* of the *1. Panzer-Division*, which operated in both the northern and central sectors of the Eastern Front in the first year of the campaign. In the first image, the *Kradschützen* pass several *Panzer III*s of *Panzer-Regiment 1*.

An *Sd.Kfz. 251/1 II (Wurfrahmen 40)* moves down a cobblestone street while efforts are made to take a built-up area. A weapons system such as this could have a devastating effect within the walled confines of city streets, providing it had a clear field of fire into the targeted area. Because of its volume of fire and high-explosive effect, accuracy was not paramount in its employment. Soldiers in the field often referred to it as the *Stuka zu Fuß* (roughly "Stuka on the ground"). The half-track has an aerial recognition panel draped over its rear, ready to be put on full display if it appears it is about to be attacked by friendly aircraft.

A *Panzer 38(t)* moves into wooded terrain behind a column of infantry. Although a tank could lend some moral support to the foot soldiers, it really was at a disadvantage when moving along narrow forest lanes, where it could be easily ambushed or halted by obstacles. The Soviet winter has at least solidified the ground somewhat, making motorized movement more feasible. Once its full fury was unleashed, however, it would play havoc with the woefully ill-prepared German forces.

FACING PAGE AND ABOVE: The Russian winter turns into bitter reality for the *Panzertruppe*. When roads weren't frozen, they were frequently quagmires of mud. Once frozen, other problems emerged: tracks frozen to the ground overnight, engines and transmissions that would not crank or turn, batteries that would not hold a charge. The cold weather was misery for the crews as well. There was no such thing as a crew heater in early tanks, and the interiors of the fighting compartments were often much colder than the ambient air temperature outside. While the Soviet forces had to deal with the same problems, they were much better prepared, with proper winter lubricants for their vehicles and warm winter uniforms for their soldiers. It is believed that these two images are from tanks of the *VI./Panzer-Regiment 3* during operations outside Moscow. The tanks of this particular company, which appear to be the *Ausführung H* of the *Panzer III*, had a stylized dragon superimposed on a variety of geometric patterns, with the circular background seen in the second image denoting the 4th Platoon. (MICHAEL H. PRUETT)

ABOVE: A company of *Panzer III*s moves out into a bleak winter landscape, with a burning village in the background. Both sides frequently burned down villages whenever forced to withdraw so as to deny even rudimentary comfort to the occupying enemy forces. (MICHAEL H. PRUETT)

LEFT: A knocked-out or abandoned KV-I blends into its surroundings in a Soviet village, thanks to its coat of winter white-wash. Like the T34, the KV-I was superior to all German designs at the time and was able to engage German armor with near impunity. Its tracks were nearly twice as wide as most German tracks, substantially lowering ground pressure despite its weight and allowing it to move and maneuver in places no German armor could go. (MICHAEL H. PRUETT)

LEFT: A German supply column moves down one of the few cleared and suitable roads available to it in the Soviet Union. Due to the poor road network, elements often had to move in two or three columns abreast, sharing the road, as opposed to using neighboring secondary routes. In this particular case, it appears that at least one-way traffic is being maintained, which helps facilitate more rapid movement. (MICHAEL H. PRUETT)

BELOW: Mechanics weld parts and work on an engine in the field. Maintenance personnel often worked around the clock for extended periods in an effort to keep the badly overtaxed German fleet running. Without the indefatigable efforts of the maintenance crews, the front-line effort would have collapsed early in the war.

CHAPTER 6

The Campaign in North Africa (1941–43)

In North Africa, the Italian Army was performing even more poorly against the British than it had against the Greeks (see the chapter on the Balkans). Intending to expand his African colonies, Mussolini ordered his army to advance into Egypt, which it reluctantly did on September 13, 1940. By September 18 the sluggish advance had stalled, allowing the British to launch a counteroffensive on December 9. Facing determined and skillful troops supported by excellent artillery and heavy infantry tanks that were impervious to antitank and tank fire, the Italian forces proceeded to totally collapse.

Instead of the British operation lasting five days as originally planned, General Wavell continued the advance, taking Bardia, Tobruk, Benghazi, and, finally, Beda Fomm. Wavell's 30,000 troops took 130,000 prisoners and, on February 7, 1941, finally halted at El Agheila, having conquered most of Libya. The moment was ripe for throwing all Italian forces out of North Africa, as was already occurring in East Africa. However, substantial numbers of Wavell's troops were diverted to Greece in an ill-fated move, and the decision was made to hold the line.

Hitler's attention was firmly focused on the East, but Mussolini's problems in North Africa could not be ignored. Accordingly, a relatively small German mobile force consisting of the *5. leichte Division*, constituted from elements of the *3. Panzer-Division* and followed by the *15. Panzer-Division*, was to be sent to North Africa as a blocking force (*Sperrverband*). The formation was named the *Deutsches Afrikakorps (DAK)* and was to be commanded by the hard-charging former commander of the *7. Panzer-Division, Generalleutnant* Erwin Rommel. On February 14, 1941, the steamer *Saarfeld* disembarked the first combat units of the *5. leichte Division*—elements of *Aufklärungs-Abteilung 3 (mot), Panzerjäger-Abteilung 39*, and *I./Panzer-Artillerie-Regiment 75*—Rommel having arrived two days earlier.

The impatient, opportunistic Rommel had no intention of sitting idle. He immediately set about probing the British positions with his reconnaissance forces and their massive eight-wheeled armored cars, the *Sd.Kfz. 231 (8-Rad)* and *Sd.Kfz. 232 (8-Rad)*, particularly impressing their opposing numbers.

The armored component of the *5. leichte Division* was *Panzer-Regiment 5,* comprising some 20 *Panzer I*s, 43 *Panzer II*s, 68 *Panzer III*s (the majority of them with the 50mm main gun), and 20 *Panzer IV*s. Although the *Panzer I*s and *II*s were being phased out by then, they were still present in significant numbers. The *15. Panzer-Division* was due to arrive in Africa starting in late April 1941, and by mid-June the transfer was supposed to be complete. The division's *Panzer-Regiment 8* had 45 *Panzer II*s, 71 *Panzer III*s (with the 50mm main gun), 20 *Panzer IV*s, and 10 command tanks. The *Panzer III*s and *IV*s were more than capable of defeating the British light and cruiser tanks.

Correctly sensing that the British were in no condition to continue their advance, Rommel acted quickly and, under the guise of a reconnaissance-in-force, commenced offensive operations. Not even waiting for the arrival of the full panzer regiment of his light division, let alone the tank regiment of the *15. Panzer-Division*, he attacked the British forces of the inexperienced 2nd Armoured Division and the Australian 9th Division on March 24. Both of the Allied divisions were seriously depleted, as parts of both had been shipped to Greece and the experienced 7th Armoured Division was being rested and reconstituted in Egypt.

El Agheila quickly fell, as did Mersa Brega and Benghazi. By April 6 the Allied planned defense line at Derna was broken. The Australian 9th Division moved back into the port city of Tobruk and was surrounded there by April 11. Rommel then mounted a hasty attack on Tobruk, expecting this vital port, so important to supplying his forces, to fall quickly. However, the determined Australian infantry, backed by British artillery and 60 operational light, medium, and infantry tanks, decisively defeated the attack by some 70 German tanks, and accompanying infantry. *Maschinengewehr-Bataillon 8* was totally destroyed in the ill-fated attack.

Much to Rommel's fury, a second, more carefully planned attack was also defeated, which Rommel blamed directly on his less-than-enthusiastic Italian allies. The assault on Tobruk is an interesting case, since it represents one of the first instances of a concerted *Blitzkrieg* assault being positively repulsed. The infantry did not panic at the approach of the

armor and held their strongly fortified positions, ironically built by the Italians. The stalwart and efficient British artillery, with more than 70 medium and heavy guns, along with both antitank guns and dug-in tanks, knocked out or disabled the German armor, which was not able to maneuver with its usual freedom.

Leaving Tobruk for a later assault, the German attack continued. Operation Brevity, a counterattack by British forces that was launched on May 15, lived up to its name and lasted only 36 hours. It was a total failure. Equally disappointing was "Battleaxe," launched on June 15. Considerably reinforced by 135 of the formidable Matildas and 82 Cruisers—50 of them the new Mark IVs that proved to be both too thinly armored and mechanically unreliable—the British lost 50 percent of their armor, both knocked out and broken down, on the first day of battle. At Halfaya Pass, five of the dreaded 88mm dual-purpose guns created havoc and destroyed the majority of the heavy Matildas used in the assault.

The British persisted in trying to draw the German armor into open battle, where their more heavily armored vehicles had the upper hand. The Germans were only too aware of the deficiencies of their tanks. They preferred to lure the British armor onto prepared positions consisting of entrenched infantry, dug-in antitank guns (the 37mm *PaK 36* being largely replaced by the far more effective 50mm *PaK 38*), and hull-down tanks, backed by field guns. The British obliged by charging bravely, but recklessly, at these prepared positions, losing most of their armor in the process. The failure of "Battleaxe" and Rommel's subsequent counterattack almost surrounded the British forces, causing them to withdraw to well inside the Egyptian border.

The arrival of the *15. Panzer-Division* was finally complete by August, and the *5. leichte Division*, augmented by additional formations, was redesignated as the *21. Panzer-Division*.

The British "Crusader" offensive was ambitiously designed to both relieve Tobruk and destroy the *DAK*. The Axis forces consisted of 240 *Panzer II*s, *III*s, and *IV*s along with 150 Italian M13s and 160 of the virtually useless Italian light tanks. The British XXX Corps alone fielded 475 Cruiser and infantry tanks. The offensive was launched on November 28 and caught Rommel completely by surprise. Once again, he displayed his tactical mastery by reacting swiftly and decisively to initially contain both the offensive and the attempted breakout by the Tobruk garrison. His audacious "race to the wire" nearly surrounded and destroyed the 7th Armoured Division, which would have precipitated a catastrophe for the British.

The British then doggedly pursued a battle of attrition, with the destruction of the Axis armor left once again to British tanks rather than artillery. British tank losses were heavy, but they could afford to lose many more tanks than could Rommel. Finally, with his tank strength withering away, Rommel authorized a withdrawal that ended at El Agheila in late December 1941.

***

Resupplied by a large convoy on January 5, 1942, Rommel resumed the offensive against the overextended 8th Army on January 21, rapidly driving it back to Gazala, 30 miles west of Tobruk, by February 4. The front remained static throughout the spring, as both sides were reinforced. Determined to gain the initiative, Rommel attacked first on May 26. Of his 560 tanks, only 320 were German, mainly *Panzer III*s and *IV*s, with a small proportion of the former up-gunned to the 50mm main gun of 60 calibers. The German and Italian forces faced more than 700 British tanks, which included some 200 of the American M3 Grant/Lee tanks with their powerful 75mm guns, although they were somewhat anachronistically placed in the hull, thereby limiting their traverse.

Despite the disparity in tank strength, Rommel outflanked the heavily mined Gazala position and formed a *Kessel* (cauldron) inside British lines, withstanding heavy attacks that cost the British most of their armor. Sensing the moment when the 8th Army was at its weakest, Rommel ordered a breakout to the east that scattered the British forces. Taking no chances this time, Rommel subjected Tobruk, its original garrison largely replaced by less experienced troops, to a major assault, with the fortress surrendering on June 21. The 8th Army was forced to pull back 300 miles to the Alam Halfa–Alamein line, which was reached on June 30, 1942. This was the high-water mark of the Axis advance into Egypt.

Rommel's assault on the British Gazala–Bir Hakeim defensive position was defeated by General Auchinleck's troops. Despite this success, Auchinleck was replaced by General Bernard Montgomery, whose first order was that there would be no retreat from this position. Rommel mounted another attack with his four German and six Italian divisions on August 31, but by September 2 little progress had been made and a withdrawal was ordered.

Proving himself to be as adept at defense as attack, Rommel ordered 500,000 antitank and antipersonnel mines to be laid and the position to be heavily fortified. With the Eastern Front the first priority, there was no hope of substantial reinforcements, although the German forces in Africa—elevated to the status of an armored field army, *Panzerarmee Afrika*—had been reinforced by the reorganized *90. leichte Afrika-Division*, the *164. leichte Afrika-Division*, and *Fallschirmjäger-Brigade Ramcke*. The supply convoys were increasingly under attack by the Royal Navy and the Royal Air Force from Malta, with only a small amount of fuel and ammunition getting through to the front lines. Only 27 *Panzer IV, Ausführung F2s*, mounting the high-velocity *75mm KwK 40 L/43*, were supplied by October, along with 74 *Panzer III, Ausführung Js*, with the *50mm KwK 39 L/60*. Both tanks were capable of defeating British armor at medium to long ranges, including the M3 Grant and the newly arrived M4 Sherman. Also a potent weapon for the Germans was the tank hunter, the *Marder III*, with its potent 76mm *PaK 36(r)* capable of penetrating 79mm of armor at 1,500 meters. A total of 66 of these tank hunters were sent to North Africa by November 1942. Initially, the British thought they mounted an 88mm gun.

On October 23 Montgomery ordered the start of the El Alamein offensive, having built up a crushing superiority in numbers of troops, guns, tanks, and aircraft. The British forces amounted to 195,000 men, 908 medium and heavy artillery pieces, and 1,029 tanks, including 250 Shermans and 170 Grants. Opposing them were 50,000 Germans and

54,000 Italians. The armor available to the Axis forces consisted of 220 German and 280 Italian tanks, the latter mostly M13/40s. There were 200 German and 250 Italian artillery pieces.

The battle of El Alamein was the turning point of the war in North Africa. It was a grinding battle of attrition, with the use of artillery and infantry supported by tanks in a manner similar to the later battles of the First World War. Despite heavy losses in infantry and armor, Montgomery continued the attack, remorselessly grinding down the Axis forces. By November 2, *Panzerarmee Afrika* was down to around 30 tanks, while the 8th Army still had more than 600. Accordingly, Rommel ordered a general retreat on November 4.

Although the Germans managed to save considerable numbers of their troops, many of the Italian soldiers were left behind, as were most of the tanks and guns. The British pursuit was both cautious and hesitant, frequently held up by desperate rearguard actions. By early February 1943 *Panzerarmee Afrika* had retreated to the comparative safety of the Mareth Line in Tunisia.

***

The Operation Torch offensive, beginning with the November 8, 1942, landing at French Morocco by Patton's Allied Western Task Force, was intended to rapidly capture the port of Tunisia and cut off the German and Italian forces in Africa. However, the Germans reacted much faster than anticipated, reinforcing the Tunisian bridgehead with three divisions, two of them armored. By January 1943, 74,000 German and 26,000 Italian troops were shipped to Tunisia, and the Allied offensive stalled in the rugged hills surrounding the town.

Two units of the formidable *Panzer VI, Tiger I*, were also shipped to Tunis: *schwere Panzer-Abteilung 501* (20 *Tigers*) and *schwere Panzer-Abteilung 504* (10 *Tigers*). Although the *Tigers* knocked out large numbers of Allied tanks—estimated at more than 200—they had no significant effect on the battle for Tunisia.

The German forces did mount some spoiling offensives, most notably on November 14 against US forces at Faid Pass. A counterattack by Combat Command A of the US 1st Armored Division ended in disaster, with 44 of the 51 tanks of 3rd Battalion, 1st Armored Regiment, destroyed. Combat Command B mounted a second attack the following day. Its 2nd Battalion suffered a similar fate, with only four of its Shermans surviving. The US Army learned the hard way the same painful lesson the British took years to learn, namely that you do not recklessly charge emplaced tanks screened by anti-tank guns. In the face of increasing US Army resistance and Allied reinforcements, the Axis offensive petered out by February 21.

On March 10 a sick, weary, and disheartened Rommel departed for Germany. The 8th Army finally broke through the Mareth Line defenses on March 26 and Patton successfully attacked at Maknassy on April 12, forcing the 1st Army of Italian general Messe to retreat. The Axis's days in Tunisia were numbered and, following a further series of concentric attacks in early May, all Axis forces in Tunisia surrendered by May 13, with some 200,000 German and Italian prisoners being taken.

Although a long, often seesawing, and extremely interesting campaign, only a relatively small number of German armored and mechanized divisions were involved, including the *10. Panzer-Division*, which was belatedly shipped to Tunisia late in 1942. The life-and-death struggle of the *Wehrmacht* was taking place in the East.

Newly arrived in Tripoli, a *Panzerbefehlswagen III, Ausführung H*, of the *II./Panzer-Regiment 5* retains its European panzer dark gray paint finish. The large turret numbers—*II01*—are painted in red with a white outline. Curious onlookers, including a large contingent of Italian soldiers, line the street. (JEFF PLOWMAN/TONY ORMANDY)

ABOVE: This earlier-model *Sd.Kfz. 251*, probably an *Ausführung C*, advances along a road near an unidentified desert fort in the beginning stages of the war in North Africa. The half-track appears to have the North African color camouflage base coat of *gelbbraun* (yellow-brown) painted over the factory-applied *dunkelgrau* (dark gray). The former was applied in the field by each unit with varying results. Approximately one-third of the vehicle was also supposed to be sprayed with *graugrün* (gray-green), but it does not appear to have happened in this case. Numerous stores have been added to the exterior of the vehicle, including spare track, tow cables, and concertina wire. In addition, a large aerial recognition panel adorns the front slope of the vehicle. Of added interest is the use of the handheld signaling device by the one soldier, an indicator that this half-track may not have been outfitted with a radio for communications. The soldiers all wear the khaki-brown tropical uniform and the iconic billed field cap closely associated with soldiers of the *Deutsches Afrikakorps*.

FACING PAGE AND NEXT SPREAD: Six views of captured German self-propelled guns, the *15cm s.FH 13/1 (Sf) auf Geschützwagen Lorraine Schlepper(f) Sd.Kfz 135/1*. These guns were among the first designs to enter the German inventory for active service with divisional artillery battalions. Some 60 vehicles were initially ordered, with the first 30 going straight to Africa and divided among the *21. Panzer-Division* (two batteries), *15. Panzer-Division* (two batteries), and *90. leichte Division* (one battery) starting in the summer of 1942. The guns continued to be used until 1944, when most were lost in Normandy while serving with *Panzer-Artillerie-Regiment 155* of the reconstituted *21. Panzer-Division*. Also of interest in some of these images is the presence of British/Commonwealth armor, such as the Matilda, the Stuart, and the General Lee. In the first image, two New Zealander "Kiwis" pose on one of the captured guns, which had been issued to *Panzer-Artillerie-Regiment 155*. The large numbers painted on the gun shield were probably added by the Allies as inventory numbers. (JEFF PLOWMAN/TONY ORMANDY)

FACING PAGE BOTTOM: The three captured vehicles seen here feature a somewhat "standard" German desert camouflage pattern, most likely consisting of a base coat of *gelbbraun* with an overspray of *graugrün*, even though the camouflage scheme had been officially superseded at this point by *braun* (brown) and *grau* (gray). (JEFF PLOWMAN/TONY ORMANDY)

This *Lorraine Schlepper* gives every indication that it is still serviceable. The only German markings that appeared on these captured guns was a *Balkenkreuz* in black, outlined in white. (JEFF PLOWMAN/TONY ORMANDY)

LEFT: An entire battery of the guns appears to have been captured. In the background, the viewer can also see a number of captured self-propelled antitank guns, the *Panzerjäger 38(t) für 7.62cm PaK 36(r), Sd.Kfz. 139*, commonly referred to as the *Marder III* (Marten III). Almost 350 of the vehicles were produced from April to November 1942. The *Marder III* featured a captured Soviet 76.2mm antitank gun, which was rechambered to take German rounds. The high silhouette and thin armor were liabilities, but the Soviet antitank gun was capable of defeating any fielded Allied armor at the time. (JEFF PLOWMAN/TONY ORMANDY)

Another view of a *Lorraine Schlepper* and a *Marder III*, both of which are missing their tracks. This particular *Lorraine Schlepper* is also lacking a national insignia. (JEFF PLOWMAN/TONY ORMANDY)

RIGHT: The 15cm gun on this *Lorraine Schlepper* appears to be at maximum elevation, with the gun spade lowered, if not entirely emplaced. (JEFF PLOWMAN/TONY ORMANDY)

A forlorn-looking later-model *Panzer IV, Ausführung F2*, either knocked out or rendered inoperable by its crew. The dislodged cupola and the burned-out front roadwheels are indicative of the former, while the barrel burst suggests the latter. The turret numbers—*843*—are red, outlined in white. The *F2* variant was the first *Panzer IV* to be armed with a longer *75mm* main gun, whose performance was superior to all British/Commonwealth armor in the desert at the time. (JEFF PLOWMAN/TONY ORMANDY)

An American GI poses with a captured *Panzer II, Ausführung F,* in North Africa. Some very interesting markings appear on the side of the vehicle's turret: a stylized wolf's head and black *I1I*, indicating a vehicle serving with the headquarters of the 1st Battalion of the regiment. Efforts to identify the battalion in question have proven elusive. (JEFF PLOWMAN/TONY ORMANDY)

FACING PAGE TOP: A knocked-out *Panzer II, Ausführung F*, assigned to the staff of a panzer regiment. Of interest are the older numbers still visible on the turret—*343*—which indicate the tank was reassigned from the 3rd Company to the regiment at some point. No replacement numbers appear to have been assigned when the tank moved to the headquarters. As the *Panzer II* became increasingly obsolescent on the battlefield, it was often pulled out of harm's way into less dangerous sectors, as may have been the case here. It is possible this tank burned out, given the discoloration seen at the turret rear. (JEFF PLOWMAN/TONY ORMANDY)

FACING PAGE BOTTOM: While the Germans still classified this weapon as an antitank rifle, the *2.8cm schwere Panzerbüchse 41* had the penetrative power to match some antitank guns of larger caliber, thanks to its innovative tapered-bore design, which reduced the 28mm round to 20mm by the time it left the muzzle. Production for the gun started in 1941 but was discontinued by 1943 because of shortages in availability of tungsten for its rounds. It had a short range, but made up for it to a certain extent by its ability to penetrate up to 52mm of armor at a 60-degree slope at 500 meters. This particular gun was captured in North Africa and is displayed with some of its ammunition. (JEFF PLOWMAN/TONY ORMANDY)

BELOW: This *schwer Personenkraftwagen Typ Ford EG* field ambulance has a very interesting two-color camouflage pattern consisting of the original dark gray with desert yellow-brown spray-painted patterns. A large Red Cross is painted on the side door. (JEFF PLOWMAN/TONY ORMANDY)

ABOVE: A knocked-out *Panzer IV, Ausführung F2*, is seen at another captured equipment collection point. While the hull seems relatively intact, the main gun appears to be out of battery or sprung from its mounting and the front part of the gun cover is dislodged. This may have been done by the crew in an effort to prevent the enemy from capturing a serviceable tank. Several *Panzer III*s bring up the rear, with at least one of them missing its tracks.

FACING PAGE TOP: Additional Kiwi trophies are seen in these images: two captured *Panzer III*s of *Panzer-Regiment 8* of the *15. Panzer-Division*. The tanks are probably either the *G* or *L* variant of the *Panzer III*. In the first image, a large red *Wolfsangel* (wolf hook), which was used by the regiment as a unit insignia, has been painted on the bolt-on armor in front of the driver and radio operator stations on the hull superstructure. Field-expedient "armor" has also been added to the tank in the form of sandbags and large sections of spare track (stacked two high in front of the commander's cupola). The *Wolfsangel* is a German runic symbol that was believed to ward off wolves. (JEFF PLOWMAN/TONY ORMANDY)

FACING PAGE BOTTOM: In this side view of a second tank, we can see both the divisional insignia (viewer's left) and the *Wolfsangel* on the spaced armor gun mantlet. As with the first tank, sections of spare track have been used to provide additional armor protection. (JEFF PLOWMAN/TONY ORMANDY)

LEFT: An atmospheric shot of a gunner on an artillery piece, probably a *schwere Feldhaubitze 18*. The gunner appears to be an "old hand" in the desert, given the wear to his M40 tropical billed field cap and the *AFRIKAKORPS* sleeve band, which was generally awarded for six months of service in theater. The firing charts seen on the right were affixed directly to the side of the gun carriage to facilitate rapid firing under most engagement scenarios without recourse to manuals.

BELOW: As in most other theaters of the war, the German forces in North Africa were perennially short of equipment and made frequent use of captured vehicles. In this case, it is a British Dingo armored car, a very successful design for British and Commonwealth forces. It was fast, agile, and quiet—all hallmarks of a good reconnaissance vehicle. Judging by the elaborate tentage and the presence of Arab camp followers, the Germans have been in this encampment for some time.

RIGHT: An early *Panzer IV, Ausführung G*, prepares to move out on operations. The radio operator maintains radio watch, while the driver and tank commander confer. Of interest is the small "stepladder" on the left side of the vehicle to make mounting it from that area easier. Based on the front slope of the hull, it appears that some sort of mud paste may have been used at one point to help camouflage the vehicle.

A limbered 88mm *FlaK* makes ready to move out after an engagement. The *88* in a ground-combat role was a favorite weapon of Rommel and his commanders and a feared one for their Allied counterparts. The gun was well suited for ground combat due to its ability to defeat all Allied armor at superior ranges. One of Rommel's more famous tactical techniques was to lure Allied armor into "kill zones," where these guns, placed at the far end of the trap, could wreak havoc on an exposed armored force.

CHAPTER 7

The Campaign against the Soviet Union (1942–43)

The German summer offensive of 1942 was code-named "Case Blue" and caught the Soviet command completely off-guard. Most of the Soviet forces were positioned to defend against a continued attack toward Moscow, whereas the Germans—who had massed more than 1,000,000 men and 1,700 tanks and self-propelled guns, although some 300 were still the obsolete *Panzer I*—attacked southeast and south, intending to capture the vital Caucasus oil fields. At first, the attack went well with impressive advances and the capture of several major cities. However, there were no major encirclements with massive losses, as the Soviet forces fell back in a relatively orderly manner.

By the middle of August, the advance of *Heeresgruppe Mitte* had stalled due to the divergent objectives of both the oil fields and Stalingrad, with too few forces and logistic support to accomplish both. The story of the heroic and resolute Soviet defense of Stalingrad, subsequent trapping of the *6. Armee* commanded by *Generaloberst* von Paulus, and Zhukov's brilliant counteroffensives is well known. Urban fighting negated the German mastery of movement warfare, with tank and infantry units bled white for little gain.

When the Soviet Operations Mars and Uranus opened on November 19 and 25, there were few German tanks to oppose them. For example, the *XXXXVIII. Panzer Korps* was expected to stop the 700 T34s of the 5th Tank Army with a mere 40 tanks. Attempts to open a corridor to the beleaguered troops in Stalingrad were beaten back. The Stalingrad disaster effectively meant that the initiative was firmly in the hands of the Soviets. German losses and those of the Italian, Hungarian, and Romanian forces could not be replaced. Tanks, aircraft, trucks, and other vital military items were also pouring into the Soviet Union, mainly from the United States, as a result of the Lend-Lease Program. Particularly valuable were the superb US 6×6 trucks, with their excellent cross-country ability and heavy load-carrying capacity, allowing Soviet factories to concentrate on artillery, aircraft, and tanks.

The Soviet winter offensive of 1942–43 was just as ambitious as that of 1941–42. It intended to knock Germany out of the war or at least recover the Ukraine and, in the process, inflict crippling casualties. Had all of *Heeresgruppe A* been trapped in the Caucasus, it would have been a disaster far greater than Stalingrad, but the *1. Panzer-Armee* managed to escape, with the remainder of the field army group being trapped on the Taman Peninsula, where it resisted Soviet assaults until October 1943, when it was evacuated by sea.

Despite the serious setbacks, the Germans demonstrated that they were still the masters of maneuver warfare when they thwarted two Soviet operations, Gallup (January 29) and Star (February 2), which were intended to exploit the 600-kilometer gap between the depleted *2. Armee* to the north and the *4. Panzer-Armee* in the south. *Generalfeldmarschall* Erich von Manstein, considered Germany's foremost operational commander, commanded *Heeresgruppe Don* and was tasked with restoring a sound defensive line in that sector. Kharkov was to be defended by the powerful *II. SS-Panzer Korps* consisting of *SS-Panzergrenadier-Division "Leibstandarte Adolf Hitler," SS-Panzergrenadier-Division "Das Reich,"* and *SS-Panzergrenadier-Division "Totenkopf,"* with each of these divisions having a company of the formidable *Tiger I*.

SS-Obergruppenführer Paul Hausser, the commanding general of the *SS* corps, ordered a withdrawal from the city on February 16, in contravention of Hitler's orders. It was almost surrounded, and Hausser feared his forces would be completely cut off and destroyed. Moreover, it appeared to the Germans that the Soviets were reaching the culminating point of their offensives. Manstein intended to use his two armored corps, the *II. SS-Panzer Korps* and the *XXXXVIII. Panzer Korps*, to eliminate the Soviet spearhead and drive the advancing forces back to the River Donets, whereupon his forces would attack to the north and recapture Kharkov. Manstein's counteroffensive began on February 20. With the *Tigers* dominating the battlefield and the *Panzer IV*s able to destroy the T34s at long range, three Soviet tank corps were destroyed in a matter of days. Soviet counterattacks were brushed aside with comparative ease, as the Germans totally outmaneuvered the Soviet units.

SS-Panzergrenadier-Division "Totenkopf" cut the last lines of communication for the Soviet forces in Kharkov on March 13, and the city was retaken the next day. Manstein's offensive operations recommenced on March 15, with the *II. SS-Panzer Korps* as its spearhead. The Soviet 3rd Tank Army

was thrown back across the Donets, and the loss of Belgorod on March 18 severed the escape route of the 69th Army, which tried and failed to make a large-scale breakout over the next four days. The spring thaw ended the fighting, with the Germans not only once again escaping total destruction, but also inflicting significant casualties on their opponents. The German position in the Ukraine was still strong, and another offensive in the summer was a threat that could not be ignored.

Once again, German rapid responsiveness to changing situations, superb staff work, and effective tactical command and control proved far superior to their Soviet counterparts'. The Soviets still had a lot to learn, but they were getting much better at conducting mobile operations and would continue to improve.

The German summer offensive, unlike the first two, had strictly limited aims. It intended to pinch off the Soviet forces in the Kursk salient, causing as many casualties as possible to forestall any Soviet offensive. In the face of a resurgent Red Army and with the threat of an Allied invasion in the West, the best the Germans could hope for was a stalemate in the East and a negotiated settlement.

Operation *Zitadelle* (Citadel) has been covered in such detail that only the briefest summary is necessary. It was an unimaginative frontal assault with 770,000 troops and 2,450 tanks and assault guns. The attack was supported by 7,400 guns and mortars and launched against numerous defensive belts some 200 to 300 kilometers deep, which were manned by 1,900,000 men and more than 5,000 tanks and self-propelled guns. These were supported by more than 30,000 guns and mortars. Operation Citadel might have worked in April, as originally proposed, but by July 5 it was an offensive that no one in the German high command, from Hitler down, really wanted.

One of the reasons for the delay was the desire to use the new *Panzer V Panther*. High expectations were placed on this tank, with about 160 available on July 6. Far from being a decisive factor in the battle, the *Panther* suffered from a variety of teething troubles, with several catching fire and burning out on the way to the battlefield. By July 10 about 20 had been destroyed by enemy action, compared to some 80 in short- and long-term repair. It has been claimed that the *Panther*s destroyed some 270 Soviet tanks, some at ranges of 3,000 meters, but it was a classic example of "too little and too late." The *Panther* was to develop into one of the outstanding tanks of the war, but its battlefield debut was less than auspicious.

In the north, *Generaloberst* Model's *9. Armee* had only progressed 13 kilometers by July 10. In the same period, *Generaloberst* Hoth's *4. Panzer-Armee* advanced 32 kilometers in the south. The battle of Prokhorovka on July 12 has often been incorrectly called the greatest tank battle of the war, involving thousands of tanks. The reality is less dramatic, as the *III. Panzer Korps* and the *II. SS-Panzer Korps* fielded approximately 470 tanks and assault guns against a maximum of 870 tanks and assault guns of the 5th Guards Tank Army. German losses for the battle can be estimated as a fairly modest 54 tanks and assault guns compared to 334 Soviet tanks and assault guns. Certainly, there was no breakthrough at Prokhorovka, but there was no shattering German defeat either.

The Germans called off the offensive due to the Soviet counteroffensives, particularly in the north, where an attack was launched toward Orel, which was recaptured on August 6. A southern operation commenced on August 3, with Belgorod liberated three days later and Kharkov recaptured for the last time on August 23.

The most serious consequence of the battle of Kursk for the Germans was that the operational and strategic initiative irrevocably passed to the Soviets, with the Germans and their allies transitioning to the defensive against massive continuing Soviet advances. This was the beginning of what the Soviets called the second phase of the Great Patriotic War, where the Germans were expelled from Soviet territory.

The battle to crush Hitler's so-called Eastern Rampart, which ran along the Dnieper River, was one of the largest fought on the Eastern Front and of enormous magnitude. The Soviet intention was to liberate the Ukraine, recover the vital Donbass industrial region, and retake Kiev. To accomplish these objectives, they assembled five fronts (field army groups) consisting of 30 field armies, each comprising two to five rifle, tank, or mechanized corps, plus attached elements such as tank and artillery brigades. These ground forces were supported by five air armies. The forces totaled 2,600,000 men, 51,000 guns and mortars, 2,400 tanks and assault guns, and 2,100 combat aircraft.

The opposing German forces comprised the *2. Armee* from *Heeresgruppe Mitte*, which was commanded by *Generalfeldmarschall* von Kluge, and the *4. Panzer-Armee* and three field armies—the 1st, 6th, and 8th—of *Heeresgruppe Süd*, commanded by the brilliant tactician *Generalfeldmarschall* von Manstein. It should be noted that German field armies were theoretically twice as large as the equivalent Soviet formation, but that none of the German formations were at full strength. In all, the Germans fielded 1,240,000 men, 12,600 guns and mortars, and around 2,000 tanks and assault guns. The latter figure represents on-hand strength. In terms of combat strength, only approximately 700 tanks and 400 assault guns were actually operational on the whole of the Eastern Front. *Luftflotte 4* provided air support, but less than 300 aircraft were operational out of the 600 it had issued. The eight *Panzer* and three *Panzergrenadier* divisions of *Heeresgruppe Süd* were reduced to less than half their authorized strength, with only 10 to 30 tanks or assault guns operational per division.

The Germans were surprised by both the speed of the advance and the skillful use of mobile groups that kept them off-balance. By September 25 major Soviet bridgeheads had been established at Rzhishchev and Veliki Burkin, in advance of Manstein's mechanized formations. In all, 23 bridgeheads were eventually established across the Dnieper. The large Burkin Bridgehead was soon cordoned off by 10 German divisions, however, and the remaining bridgeheads were placed under continuous fire. Soviet general Vatutin's breakout attempts cost the Red Army considerable tank and infantry casualties. Conversely, the German forces were not strong enough to eliminate these bridgeheads, despite considerable reinforcements from the west, including substantial numbers of *Tigers* and *Panthers*, with all attempts ending with irreplaceable losses in tanks and infantry. The *Panther*s were still proving to be prone to numerous mechanical breakdowns, thereby nullifying their role in establishing armored supremacy over the now inadequately armed and armored T34s.

On October 15 there was a major breakout from the Myshuryn Rog Bridgehead. The Germans had been focusing instead on the Burkin Lodgement. A major counteroffensive by the new commanding general of the XXXX. *Panzer Korps, General* Ferdinand Schörner, who had no experience in the Ukraine or of large-scale armored operations, was mounted near Krivoi Rog from October 28 to 31. The German forces included six *Panzer* divisions, three *Panzergrenadier* divisions, and *schwere Panzer-Abteilung 506,* with its *Tiger I*s. Schörner largely bungled the operation, much to the chagrin of Manstein, by starting the attack before all his tanks had arrived and attacking the salient frontally instead of mounting a pincer operation against the base. The attack did, however, seal a serious breach in the German front, but this respite was only temporary.

As was increasingly the case, Hitler demanded that his battered and outnumbered formations hold their positions along the thinly manned front, even to the extent of ordering the IV. and XXIX. *Armee-Korps* with their eight divisions to maintain the Nikopol Bridgehead on the east bank of the Dnieper in order to protect the manganese mines on the west bank. The Soviet bridgeheads could only be contained for so long, and on November 3 a major breakout from the Lyutezh Bridgehead was made with substantial tank and mechanized formations, including Rybalko's 3rd Guards Tank Army. For once, the Germans reacted slowly to this threat, and the speed and proficiency of the advance caught them by surprise. By November 6 Kiev had been liberated, and the following day the critical rail junction at Fastov was captured. On the 13th of the same month, the equally crucial rail junction at Zhitomir was taken, seriously disrupting German reinforcements from the West and causing a crisis for *Heeresgruppe Süd.*

A counterattack by the XXXXVIII. *Panzer Korps* recaptured Zhitomir on November 20, causing heavy Soviet casualties, particularly Rybalko's armor, and averting a serious situation for *Heeresgruppe Süd.* However, there were no large-scale encirclements and disorganized retreats, as the Red Army was now experienced in reacting to and countering German attacks. In the south, the Soviet advance was slow and costly, with the Germans mounting a number of successful counterattacks. The Nikopol Bridgehead, defended by nine infantry divisions and the 24. *Panzer-Division*, continued to hold out against no less than four Soviet field armies.

Finally, on December 24, Vatutin's 1st Ukrainian Front attacked the XXXXII. *Armee-Korps* with overwhelming strength, and it soon started to collapse. By December 29 there was no continuous German front, and the 4. *Panzer-Armee* was effectively shattered. Konev's forces advanced 30 kilometers in five days, coming close to destroying Wöhler's 8. *Armee.* The situation toward the end of December was critical for *Heeresgruppe Süd*, with the Red Army resuming the offensive, almost without pause.

Soviet losses were more than 1,000,000 men, with 290,000 dead or missing, and some 12,000 armored vehicles, but both personnel and equipment could be replaced, particularly as new recruits were now available from the Ukrainian populace. *Heeresgruppe Süd* suffered 370,000 casualties, with 100,000 dead or missing, and these could not be effectively replaced. German tank losses were about a fifth of the Red Army's, but the Soviet Union was outproducing Germany on a massive scale, with some 20,000 Russian tanks built compared to some 6,000 German. It was also aided by Lend-Lease tanks and trucks from the United States.

What the Dnieper campaign convincingly demonstrated was that the Red Army was now capable of mounting and, more importantly, sustaining large-scale combined-arms operations simultaneously and on multiple fronts, employing massive infantry, artillery, tank, and air superiority. The Dnieper campaign set the basic pattern for all subsequent Soviet offensive operations: multiple attacks along an extended front, rapid reinforcement of breakthroughs, and the use of large mobile groups to disrupt and unhinge the defense, all combined with very effective tactical air support.

Weary soldiers man a *MG34* on a tripod in a static defensive position. After the brutal winter of 1941–42, the Germans manned static defensive positions along the Eastern Front until the spring thaw and mud period were over, the forces in the field had had a chance to recuperate and conduct at least rudimentary battlefield reconstitutions, and the high command was able to decide its operational objectives for the summer offensives. While the motorized infantry forces and the fledgling mechanized infantry—the *Panzergrenadier*—frequently rode to the battlefield, they were often indistinguishable from their traditional "leg" counterparts once battle was joined or in static defensive positions. The tripod-mounted machine gun provided several advantages for defensive fighting: greater stability, the capability of firing without exposing the crew, and greater range (if additional telescopic sights were mounted). (MICHAEL H. PRUETT)

TOP: Once the summer offensive got under way—with its main effort, *Schwerpunkt*, in the south—scenes reminiscent of Operation Barbarossa began to be replayed, with crowded roads and towering clouds of blinding road dust. Although this image of *Sd.Kfz. 251*s of *Panzer-Pionier-Bataillon 16*, the divisional armored combat engineers of the *16. Panzer-Division,* was taken in 1941, it easily could have been a year later. Based on the frames seen on the two half-tracks, these are probably *Sd.Kfz. 251 II*s with the *Wurfrahmen 40* rocket-launcher system mounted on the sides.

BOTTOM: This *Sd.Kfz. 251 II* was assigned to *Pionier-Bataillon 40* of the *24. Panzer-Division*, as can be ascertained by the divisional insignia—the *springende Reiter* (Leaping Horseman)—on the right front side. The division had been the *1. Kavallerie-Division*, which still owed its mobility in large part to horse mounts, before it was withdrawn in late 1941 and reconstituted as an armored division. Despite that, the East Prussian division still maintained proud ties to its horse cavalry tradition.

In the spring of 1942, the short-barreled *Panzer IVs* began to be replaced by new variants featuring guns of longer caliber, starting with the *Ausführung F2*, which mounted a *Kraftwagenkanone 40 L43* that had nearly twice the velocity of the older main gun of 24 calibers. These changes were necessitated by the dynamic of warfare design and development, which saw each side developing larger and larger weapons systems with increasing lethality. In this image, we see both the older and newer versions of the *Panzer IV* side by side. The *Panzer IV, Ausführung F2,* can be easily identified by its ball-shaped muzzle brake.

ABOVE AND FACING PAGE TOP: In the early part of the summer offensive, even some combat elements had difficulty maintaining the pace of the advance. Artillery elements such as these seemed to spend most of their time limbered and on the move. The prime movers for the *schwere Feldhaubitze 18* are the *Mittlerer Zugkraftwagen 8t Sd.Kfz. 7.*

FACING PAGE BOTTOM: These *Panzergrenadier* elements, riding in early production models of the *Sd.Kfz. 251*, cross a ford site marked by engineers. When combat elements encountered water obstacles, they sometimes "stacked up" at the crossing sites since there were usually not enough crossings across the front lines to accommodate all traffic simultaneously. As a result, elements frequently had to go out of sector to cross an obstacle and then rely on lead elements to open up the bridgehead to allow continued operations. It looks as though the combat engineers may be constructing a bridge off to the viewer's right, based on the presence of the pneumatic raft in the water.

Scouts from an unidentified reconnaissance element in images with the tracked vehicle most closely associated with them: the *Sd.Kfz. 250*. In this case, the half-track is among the early production variants, referred to as the *alt* (old), and features a multi-angled shape that was later streamlined to simplify construction. In the first image, the scouts take a break in heavily vegetated terrain.

A typical unimproved Soviet road after a downpour. Most of the scouts have taken refuge on their vehicle, while one remains on the ground in the ankle-deep mud, which covers the lower hull of the *Sd.Kfz. 250.*

A fine layer of mud covers the front part of the *Sd.Kfz. 250*, providing additional camouflage in the dense vegetation. Despite the primitive conditions, the soldiers put on a brave face.

Scouts take a moment to pose next to the burned-out remnants of a destroyed Soviet freight train.

Heavily camouflaged *Sd.Kfz. 250*s of the reconnaissance battalion of the *7. Panzer-Division, Kradschützen-Bataillon 7*, move across open terrain. As the division was pulled out of the front lines in May 1942 to conduct a reconstitution in France, this scene may be of training conducted while there in the summer of that year.

An *SS* soldier from one of the *Panzergrenadier* regiments of *SS-Division "Das Reich"* poses with an airman from the *Luftwaffe* in a staff car of the battalion headquarters. The *Kübelwagen* (literally "bucket car") was the equivalent of the US Army's jeep. Like the *7. Panzer-Division*, the *SS*-division was moved to France in early 1942 to undergo reconstitution. It was also reorganized there and was redesignated as *SS-Panzergrenadier-Division "Das Reich."* This image may stem from that period, given the pristine condition of the *Kübelwagen*, although the architecture in the background suggests somewhere in the Soviet Union. The color also appears to be almost too dark to be the standard dark gray.

FACING PAGE TOP: An up-armored *Panzer III*, *Ausführung F*, armed with the *5cm Kampfwagenkanone L42*, of *Panzer-Regiment 4* of the *13. Panzer-Division*, appears to be broken down somewhere along a forlorn stretch of roadway in the southern part of the Soviet Union. The division had the distinction of being part of the farthest advance to the east that the Germans conducted during the war against the Soviet Union, although that achievement was relatively short-lived after the debacle at Stalingrad and the entire German southern front had to be pulled back. Of interest with this *Panzer III* is the white divisional marking on the front glacis of the tank near the driver's station and the flying of a small party pendant from the vehicle's radio antenna. A "tanker's bar" rests near the left drive sprocket, indicating that there is some sort of running gear issue. Due to the hot weather, which could cause temperatures inside the vehicles to soar, the crew typically removed their hot wool panzer jackets. In addition, all hatches of the vehicle tended to remain open for as long as possible.

FACING PAGE BOTTOM: This *Sd.Kfz. 251, Ausführung C,* rolls across open terrain somewhere in the Soviet Union. Given the wearing of the field caps, the lack of weapons, and the partial covering of the open rear compartment with a tarpaulin, the half-track is probably somewhere in a rear area, perhaps undergoing a test run after a repair or main-tenance has been performed. This vehicle features an unusual field-applied camouflage pattern, which appears to be splotches of *dunkelgelb* (dark yellow) paint over a base coat of *dunkelgrau* (dark gray). Also of interest is the mounting of a spare roadwheel on the left front superstructure, something usually not seen on half-tracks.

BELOW: A *Waffen-SS* crew member poses behind his *3.7cm FlaK 36*, which is mounted on what appears to be a 5-ton prime mover, the *Sd.Kfz. 6/2*. On the wide-open steppes of the Soviet Union, there was generally no concealment offered from aerial obser-vation, although that was less of a concern to antiaircraft crews since they wanted to draw out enemy aircraft to engage them. Ammunition can be seen on the ready racks next to the gun, and additional ammunition canisters are arrayed along the sides of the rear platform of the vehicle. The weapon could fire at a sustained rate of 120 rounds a minute. (MICHAEL H. PRUETT)

LEFT: This NCO of the *3. SS-Panzergrenadier-Division "Totenkopf"* demonstrates his front-line ingenuity. While his *Sd.Kfz. 251, Ausführung D,* serves as shelter, a cookstove has been constructed. Empty wooden ammunition crates, a water-filled bucket, and a blowtorch are then used to cook the crew's meal of potatoes or eggs. Like the *SS* soldiers seen in the previous image, he wears a camouflage smock over his field uniform. (MICHAEL H. PRUETT)

FACING PAGE TOP: This Model 1941 T34/76 with steel roadwheels and a cast turret—hallmarks of Factory 183—was captured by the Germans around Woronesch and impressed into service. It appears to have retained its original Soviet green paint but with the addition of an oversize simple white *Balkenkreuz*. As always, captured enemy equipment draws in military "sightseers."

FACING PAGE BOTTOM: *SS* combat engineers observe a village aflame as they pass by in their *Sd.Kfz. 251/7*, the combat engineer version of the half-track, which carried sections of assault bridge on each side of the super-structure. The *MG42*, seen here on a pedestal mount on the rear of the vehicle, began being issued to the field in 1942, intended as a replacement for the *MG34*. The *SS* were among the first combat forces to routinely wear camouflaged uniforms, as seen here with the use of helmet covers and smocks.

A *schwerer Zugkraftwagen 12t (Sd.Kfz. 8)* of the *Luftwaffe* pulls a limbered 88mm *FlaK* along an unimproved road in a Soviet village. The half-track crew has installed the canvas cover over the vehicle and the gun has a tarpaulin shroud over its breech, perhaps in an effort to keep road dust off the crew and the firing mechanism of the gun. The *88* continued to be a formidable weapon until the end of the war and was highly valued by ground commanders for its ability to help keep enemy armor at bay. The unit emblem on the rear of the half-track has yet to be identified.

TOP: A pair of freshly whitewashed *Panzer IV, Ausführung G,* medium tanks on a Soviet street. It was a unit responsibility to apply whitewash in the field, which resulted in a great deal of variance in its application. In this case, a uniform coat seems to have been applied over the entire vehicle. In many instances, camouflage patterns were applied by brush or spray guns in varying degrees of intensity and inventiveness. The advantage of whitewash was that it quickly wore off the vehicles with the change of seasons and several rainstorms. Although winter camouflage could be effective in snow-covered open terrain, it offered little concealment in built-up areas.

BOTTOM: This *Panzer III, Ausführung J,* of *Panzer-Regiment 24* of the *24. Panzer-Division* takes shelter next to a Soviet outbuilding in late fall during its drive on Stalingrad. The winter of 1942–43 would prove almost as harsh as the one that preceded it.

ABOVE: Maintenance personnel perform an arduous task under primitive conditions: changing an engine in the open on a bleak winter's day. The maintenance *Sd.Kfz. 9/1* has a 3-ton Bilstein crane for doing repairs such as these. The *Panzer III* undoubtedly belongs to *Panzer-Regiment 15* of the *11. Panzer-Division*, as indicated by the unit marking on the back of the half-track. Of interest is the use of winter tracks on the tank, which was accomplished by the fitting of extensions on the regular track. This effectively decreased the ground pressure of the vehicle, allowing it more maneuverability in deep snow. The winter tracks were referred to by the Germans as *Ostketten* (eastern tracks) and used extensively on armored fighting vehicles based on the *Panzer III* and *Panzer IV* chassis until 1944, when wider track was also developed and fielded for those vehicles.

FACING PAGE TOP: A somewhat glum-looking crew and comrades from *Kradschützen-Bataillon 7* of the *7. Panzer-Division* poses on an *Sd.Kfz. 263 (8-Rad)* in the winter of 1942–43. The vehicle has received an overall coat of whitewash, which appears to have been applied over a base coat of *dunkelgrau*. Of interest are the extra stores carried on the vehicle, including two spare tires, at least two 20-liter fuel cans, and a large storage box on the rear deck. In April 1943 the motorcycle infantry battalion was reorganized and redesignated as *Panzer-Aufklärungs-Abteilung 7*.

FACING PAGE BOTTOM: *Panzer VIs* of an unknown unit are loaded on railcars for transport. The vehicles are painted in overall panzer gray, indicating one of the earlier battalions to be equipped with the *Tiger*. Despite a common misconception that these vehicles were produced in great numbers and formed the mainstay of German armored forces toward the end of the war, less than 1,350 of the *Tiger Is* were manufactured. They were assigned almost exclusively to corps-level separate heavy tank battalions and used somewhat sparingly as a *Schwerpunkt* weapon. The *Panzer VI* was the first German tank to mount the 88mm weapon as a main gun. Crewed by five men, it was somewhat ponderous and overengineered, but it was feared on the battlefield due to its excellent armor protection and the lethality of its main gun. It began to be replaced in late 1944 by its next variant, the *Tiger II*.

In this image, the *Tigers* have been loaded on the railcars with their so-called "combat" tracks; that is, the tracks normally used in the field. A second set of tracks, referred to as "transport" tracks, also accompanied the battalions. These were normally mounted during rail movements, since they provided the tank with a much narrower profile. In this case, the urgency of the movement must have outweighed the need for safety, and the transport tracks have been placed under the tanks for shipment. (MICHAEL H. PRUETT)

ABOVE: The year 1943 saw the introduction of the second-most-famous tank in the German inventory during the war, the *Sd.Kfz. 171 Panzer V "Panther."* The initial version, the *Ausführung D*, which is generally recognizable by its drum-shaped commander's cupola, had a production run of almost 850 from January to September 1943. Because of its hasty design—due in large part to the surprise appearance of the T34 on the battlefield—the vehicle suffered from many teething problems, foremost among them mechanical problems due to overheating engines, fuel leaks, and transmission and final drive failures. These early production issues were largely overcome with subsequent variants—the *Ausführung A* and the *Ausführung G*—and the tank was later regarded as one of the finest medium tanks of World War II. In all, the Germans produced nearly 7,000 combat and combat-support vehicles using the *Panther* chassis, third in line after the *Sturmgeschütz III* (around 9,400 units) and the *Panzer IV* (almost 8,300 units).

In this image, a *Panzer V, Ausführung D*, of the *2./Panzer-Abteilung 51* moves past the wreckage of a destroyed Russian vehicle during Operation *Zitadelle*. The white-outlined black tactical numbers *241* indicate this to be the vehicle of the platoon leader of the 4th Platoon. Notice that this vehicle lacks the panther-head unit emblem, which can be partially seen in the next two images. Judging from period photographs of *Panzer-Regiment von Lauchert* (*Panzer-Abteilung 51* and *Panzer-Abteilung 52*), the ad hoc tank regiment formed just for employment in the operation; the panther-head unit emblem varied with each company, and its use would appear to be sporadic at best. (MICHAEL H. PRUETT)

FACING PAGE BOTTOM: In the next image, *Panther 342* has a number of interesting features. It is painted in overall dark yellow, with an irregularly applied green camouflage overspray. The vehicle numbers, painted in red, appear on the upper front portion of the turret. The black-outlined panther-head unit emblem is partially obscured from view by the metal carrying case for the M1924 stick grenade hung on the turret side. A light coat of mud covers the running gear. The crew appears to have made itself at home, draping tarpaulins and shelter halves over the rear deck and extending out from the rear of the tank, where fuel cans, ammunition crates, and an assortment of odds and ends can be seen. In the background, a *Ferdinand* of *schwere Panzerjäger-Abteilung 654* can be seen on a separate railway line. (MICHAEL H. PRUETT)

Armored vehicles moving down a city street draw curious onlookers in this prewar image. In the lead is a *Panzer IV, Ausführung C*, of which approximately 140 vehicles were made starting in 1938. It is followed by what appears to be a *Panzer I, Ausführung A*, which has had its turret and superstructure removed to create a field-expedient driver-training vehicle. These conversions were authorized in late 1937 to be performed by regimental maintenance sections to facilitate driver training. The *Panzer IV* shows the prewar and early war two-tone camouflage of two-thirds No. 46 Dark Gray (*dunkelgrau Nr. 46*) and one-third No. 45 Dark Brown (*dunkelbraun Nr. 45*). Introduced in July 1937, the scheme was used until June 1940, when armored vehicles were to be painted solely in *dunkelgrau*. The grayscale insert of the same image shows how difficult it is to determine whether early war vehicles were painted in the two-tone pattern. Also of interest in this image is the "panther" (or possibly cheetah) on the front glacis of the *Panzer IV*. It appears to have been applied in black paint with a dark yellow outline. From a uniform perspective, the headphones the *Panzer IV* commander is wearing appear to have orange-colored ear cushions, as opposed to the natural rubber appearance of the standard-issue ones.

This image and all of the remaining ones in this section appear courtesy of Akira Takiguchi. The images are all reproduced from original color-slide film and have not been colorized. The grayscale inserts are provided to show how camouflage colors are often difficult to ascertain, given the color-masking properties of period black-and-white imagery. (AKIRA TAKIGUCHI)

Regimental headquarters section vehicles line up for a parade somewhere in prewar Germany. The *Sd.Kfz. 265 kleiner Panzerbe-fehlswagen I* was the first large-scale attempt at producing a command and control vehicle for the *Panzertruppe*, and approximately 180 were produced out of various production runs of the light tank, with these command tanks appearing to have the last type of commander's cupola fitted to them. *Sd.Kfz. 265*s were issued to headquarters elements starting in late 1936. As in the previous plate, the vehicles have been painted with the two-tone camouflage scheme, thus dating the image to July 1937, at the earliest. The *Panzer II* appears to be an early production variant of the vehicle, either the *Ausführung A* or *B*. The commander of this vehicle has the honor of being the regimental standard-bearer. In addition to his regulation panzer uniform, he wears a standard-bearer's sash and gorget and carries the cased regimental colors. (AKIRA TAKIGUCHI)

Early-model *Sd.Kfz. 251* half-tracks of the *16. Panzer-Division* are seen halted in a field somewhere in the Soviet Union, probably in 1941. The half-tracks are painted in an overall *Nr. 46 dunkelgrau*, which officially became *RAL 7021 dunkelgrau* in February 1941. Since none of the personnel are wearing helmets, this might be a training exercise. When looking at the grayscale insert, the dark gray color of the vehicles stands out, but it would be difficult to tell whether there was also dark brown present, unless the viewer knew other details such as date, location, or vehicular variant. (AKIRA TAKIGUCHI)

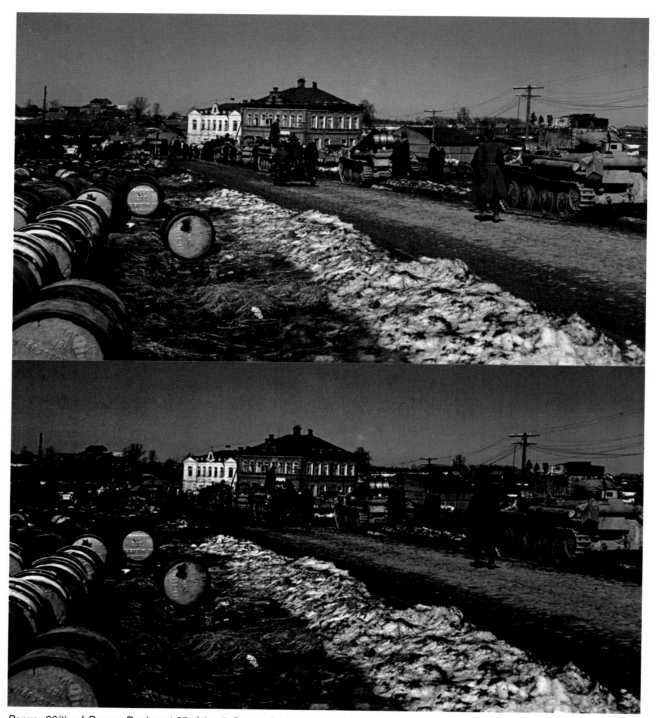

*Panzer 38(t)*s of *Panzer-Regiment 25* of the *7. Panzer-Division* somewhere in the Soviet Union, probably late winter 1941–42 or early spring 1942. In May of 1942 the division was pulled out of the line for reconstitution in France, where it traded in its *Panzer 38(t)*s for German tanks. The vehicles show signs of hard campaigning, including a weather-beaten appearance, large amounts of external storage, and the mounting of ditching beams along the hull sides. The whitewash that had been applied in the winter has largely worn away, exposing the *dunkelgrau* base coat underneath. The vehicles appear to be halted for fuel, as evidenced by the large number of 200-liter fuel drums next to the road. This particular image was taken by a soldier assigned to *Kraftfahr-Abteilung 562*, a transportation battalion. (AKIRA TAKIGUCHI)

A staff car of *Propaganda-Kompanie 697* struggles to negotiate the seemingly bottomless mud of an unimproved Soviet road during a spring thaw or a fall mud season. A soldier or war correspondent hangs on to a running board of the vehicle, prepared to jump off into the muck in case a push is needed. Based on the headgear, this image was taken in the Soviet Union sometime in 1941 or 1942. (AKIRA TAKIGUCHI)

Three *Panzer IV, Ausführung F1*, tanks of *Panzer-Regiment 31* of the *5. Panzer-Division* at some sort of staging area in a Soviet village, as evidenced by the tentage and the placement of a bipod-mounted *MG34* on the turret roof of the foreground tank. The *F1* variant of the *Panzer IV* was produced from April 1941 to March 1942 and some 471 were manufactured. The foreground tank is painted in overall *dunkelgrau*, although its main gun has a yellowish ring about mid-barrel and the aerial deflector also appears to be a shade of *dunkelgelb*, indicating the tank was originally painted that color. The second *Panzer IV* almost appears to have a later-war three-tone camouflage of red-brown (*rotbraun*), dark yellow (*dunkelgelb*), and olive green (*olivgrün*), although none of that can be seen in the grayscale insert image. It is believed the image was actually taken in 1942, which would predate the official introduction of the three-tone camouflage scheme by nearly a year. Support vehicles of the regiment can be seen in the background. This photograph was originally taken by a war correspondent assigned to *Propaganda-Kompanie 697*. (AKIRA TAKIGUCHI)

A relatively new *Panzer IV, Ausführung F2*, possibly shortly after its issuance to *Panzer-Regiment 29* of the *12. Panzer-Division,* as evidenced by its overall condition and the muzzle cover in its main gun. It features a two-tone camouflage pattern consisting of what appears to be a base coat of *dunkelgelb* with some variation of green in splotches. That opens the possibility that the vehicle had been intended for Africa—where similar camouflage schemes had been introduced, such as *grünbraun* (green-brown) and *khakhi-grau* (khaki-gray)—but the vehicle was never sent there due to the deteriorating situation. The main gun seems to have retained its gray heat-resilient primer, indicating a possible barrel change with a replacement barrel, which was never painted in camouflage colors. As with the previous images, the two-tone camouflage scheme is much harder to discern when the image is rendered in black-and-white. (AKIRA TAKIGUCHI)

A mid-production *Jagdpanther* is seen maneuvering for propaganda purposes at Mailly-le-Camp in France during the new-equipment training of *schwere Panzerjäger-Abteilung 654* in 1944. Although many images were taken for official purposes, this particular shot was in the personal possession of a soldier assigned to the battalion, Siegfried Keller. It is not known whether he took the photograph. The *Jagdpanther* features the three-tone camouflage scheme that was introduced in 1943. Of interest is the fact that the vehicle commander wears a custom-made panzer jacket in the army water-pattern camouflage pattern. (AKIRA TAKIGUCHI)

LEFT: Photographed just following Operation *Zitadelle*, two *Panther*s of the *3./Panzer-Abteilung 51* are seen while in transport. It is possible that these are 2 of the 16 *Panther*s that were to be returned to Germany for major overhaul in late July 1943. *Panther 335* appears painted in an overall *dunkelgelb* (dark yellow), which was the factory-finish base coat starting in 1943. Although difficult to see, a black-outlined panther-head unit emblem appears below the vehicle numbers. Several hits to the front plate can be observed, as well as an additional set of tracks stowed under the vehicle. The frontal armor of the *Panther* was invulnerable to all Soviet tank and antitank guns of the period. Even the 85mm gun of the T34/85 could not penetrate the sloped front plate.

ABOVE: In this image, a *schwerer Zugkraftwagen 12t (Sd.Kfz. 8)* with a limbered 88mm *FlaK* passes a broken-down *Panzerjäger Tiger (P)*, more commonly referred to as the *Ferdinand* in honor of its designer, *Professor* Ferdinand Porsche. The 88mm gun has been covered in field-expedient natural foliage as additional camouflage over what appears to be the dark gray with dark yellow overspray paint job it shares with its prime mover. The great variety in the application of camouflage can easily be seen when they are compared to the *Ferdinand*, which has a dark yellow base with large green overspray splotches. The *Ferdinand* was another example of German overengineering, with electrically powered final drives, twin engines, and two drive sprockets (the forward ones for the brakes and the rearward ones for the final drives). The vehicle was a highly effective tank-killer, combining thick armor and a potent 88mm antitank gun of 71 calibers, but a nightmare to maintain and recover. Most of the losses sustained were due to breakdowns and the inability to recover stranded vehicles whenever the Germans were forced to pull back. The upgraded version of the vehicle, which saw action in Italy and on the Eastern Front, was known as the *Elefant* (Elephant), but many of its design problems were never adequately addressed.

FACING PAGE TOP: Close-up view of the driver of a Borgward *B IVc* demolition charge carrier. These vehicles were assigned to radio-controlled tank battalions, *Panzer-Abteilungen (Funklenk)*. Conceptually, the vehicle was driven to a target area, whereupon the driver dismounted and guided the unmanned vehicle to a target via a radio-control transmitter. The vehicle then placed a 450-kilogram charge on the target and was guided back to the driver's area for subsequent use. The charge was also remotely detonated. In practice, the radio-control units proved unreliable in service, and the relatively large size of the carrier made it easy to spot and engage on the battlefield as it approached its target. Despite that, some 305 units were produced from late 1943 through late 1944. In this image, a metal bracket has been added to the left side of the vehicle to hold the driver's detachable front armor plate when not in use. As was typical for the late 1943 time period, this crewman wears the black panzer overseas cap with the first-pattern panzer denim uniform in reed-green herringbone twill. (MICHAEL H. PRUETT)

FACING PAGE BOTTOM: This *Panzer V, Ausführung D,* from an unknown unit was apparently photographed in the Kiev area in 1943. It features *Zimmerit* that was most likely applied in the field, since the order to apply it at the factories was not issued until the *A* version of the tank had started to be manufactured.

The crew of this *Sturmgeschütz III, Ausführung G,* converses with the commanding general of an army corps. It would appear that it is *General der Gebirgstruppe* Ferdinand Schörner, who commanded the *XXXX. Panzer korps* from November 1943 through January 1944. Notice that the assault gun crewmen wear black M43 panzer caps, when they would normally wear the field-gray variant, unless this happens to be part of a panzer unit that was issued assault guns, a common occurrence in the latter half of the war. The assault gun features a worn coating of whitewash and a partial set of sideskirts, which were designed to be a form of stand-off armor to defeat Soviet antitank rifle rounds. While effective at doing that, the thin sheet metal was easily dislodged or torn off under field conditions. The assault gun also features the so-called waffle-pattern *Zimmerit.* (KEN NIEMAN)

CHAPTER 8

The Campaign in Italy (1943–45)

On July 10, 1943, the Allies landed in Sicily with eight divisions of the US 7th Army, commanded by General George Patton, and the British 8th Army, commanded by General Bernard Montgomery. This was three more divisions than were landed on June 6, 1944, at Normandy.

Patton's 7th Army landed on the western end of Sicily and Montgomery's forces on the east coast. The backbone of the German defense was *Fallschirm-Panzer-Division "Hermann Göring"* and the *15. Panzergrenadier-Division.* Between the two divisions, they fielded 52 *Panzer III*s (3 with 75mm L/24), 78 *Panzer IV*s, and 29 *StuG III*s. Also attached to the German forces was the *2./schwere Panzer-Abteilung 504* with 17 *Tiger I*s. After the invasion, the *1. Fallschirm-Jäger-Division* and the *29. Panzergrenadier-Division* (with 43 *StuG. III*s) were sent as reinforcements.

Montgomery's forces slowly advanced up the east coast while Patton, showing his customary dash, rapidly advanced on Palermo. On July 20 Patton was ordered to advance to the east in order to outflank the German divisions holding up Montgomery's advance past Mount Etna. Once this was accomplished, Patton continued his rapid advance. By this time, however, the Axis forces were already preparing to quit the island.

After a hard-fought delaying action, the Germans began a brilliantly executed evacuation to the Italian mainland across the Strait of Messina. Despite the overwhelming Allied air and naval superiority, 130,000 German and Italian troops were successfully ferried to Italy with almost all their heavy equipment. This was accomplished under a massive antiaircraft umbrella and extensive sea-mine barriers.

By the time Patton's troops entered Messina on August 17, the Axis forces were safely in Italy, where they contributed significantly to its defense. Although proclaimed a major Allied victory, questions needed to be asked as to how two understrength German armored divisions with minimal reinforcements and a handful of *Tigers*, held off two Allied field armies, enjoying massive land and air superiority for more than a month.

The invasion of Europe proper began on September 3, 1943, when Montgomery's 8th Army landed at Reggio di Calabria across from Messina, followed by smaller landings at various points on the coast. The Italian government of Badoglio signed an armistice with the Allies on the same day, but it was not announced publicly until five days later. On September 8 the US 15th Army, commanded by General Mark Clark, landed at Salerno with six US and British divisions, along with rangers and commandos.

The British landing was largely unopposed, with the Germans staging a retrograde operation, demolishing roads and bridges in the process. The situation at Salerno was quite different, however, as the Germans reacted with their customary swiftness. A battle group of *Fallschirm-Panzer-Division "Hermann Göring,"* the *16. Panzer-Division*, the *26. Panzer-Division*, the *15. Panzergrenadier-Division*, and the *29. Panzergrenadier-Division* rapidly moved to seal off the landing zone, with the intent of throwing the invading forces back into the sea. This objective was nearly accomplished, with Allied airpower and naval gunfire breaking up the largest counterattack on September 13. The beachhead was completely consolidated on September 18, after linking up with Montgomery's forces two days earlier.

The Germans slowly withdrew to the formidable Gustav Line, which was 15 kilometers deep in some sectors. The numerous difficult river crossings and skillful delaying actions by the Germans slowed the Allied advance to a crawl, and it was only in December that the Allies even reached the Gustav Line proper.

The Gustav Line constituted a formidable barrier, particularly the defenses at Monte Cassino, which guarded the approaches to the Liri Valley, seen as the gateway to Rome. The resolute defenders of the town of Cassino were the tough paratroopers of the *1. Fallschirm-Jäger-Division,* backed by the *90. Panzergrenadier-Division*. One of the most effective fortifications emplaced in the Gustav Line was the *Pantherturm I* and *II, Panther* turrets on either steel, concrete, or wooden bases, positioned where their long-range firepower was most effective. These turrets were from the *A* and *D* versions of the tank and often specially modified with 65mm roof armor, making them practically invulnerable to plunging artillery fire, even of heavy caliber. Presenting a low profile, these dug-in turrets

accounted for numerous Allied tanks, even the heavily armored British Churchill with its 152mm of frontal armor.

In order to outflank the Gustav Line, an amphibious operation was launched by the US VI Corps at Anzio on January 21, 1944. The landing achieved complete surprise with no opposition, stunning the Germans. However, instead of immediately striking inland, the corps commander consolidated a shallow bridgehead of only 10 kilometers. Once again, the ability of the Germans to react rapidly was critically underestimated, as *Generalfeldmarschall* Kesselring rushed largely ad hoc forces to the landing site to contain the bridgehead. As soon as sufficient reinforcements arrived, including the *16. SS-Panzergrenadier-Division "Reichsführer SS,"* a major counterattack was mounted on February 15. It almost broke through to the coast, but was finally halted by bombing and artillery and naval gunfire. Kesselring was content to then seal off the bridgehead, keeping it under continuous heavy fire, with even the depleted *Luftwaffe* units putting in an appearance, including the innovative use of guided bombs and missiles against naval targets. The Germans derisively referred to Anzio as the world's largest self-sustaining prisoner-of-war camp.

The substantially reinforced US VI Corps, now commanded by Major General Lucian Truscott, finally broke out on May 23 as part of Operation Diadem. On May 26, one day after Truscott's forces linked up with the 5th Army, Clark attacked toward Rome rather than northeast, allowing the *10. Armee* to employ delaying tactics and eventually escape with most of its men and equipment. Clark has been rightly criticized for allocating priority to the liberation of Rome, which US troops entered on June 4, rather than seeking to destroy the *10. Armee*. In any event, the capture of Rome was totally overshadowed two days later by the successful invasion of Normandy.

Kesselring astutely had his forces fall back on a series of intermediate positions before occupying his last line of defense in Italy, the Gothic Line. Established between Pisa and Rimini, it was occupied on August 4 with little interference from the Allies. By this stage a number of Allied divisions and commanders such as Montgomery had been transferred back to England and North Africa in order to take part in Operation Overlord, the invasion of Normandy, and Operation Dragoon, the invasion of southern France.

The Allies again bogged down on the Gothic Line, with appalling weather playing a large part. The Germans had reinforced their defenses there with eight divisions, four of them from the Eastern Front. Only the depleted *26. Panzer-Division* remained on the front line, with two more panzer divisions in reserve. The Allies first attacked the Gothic Line on August 25, with the US VI Corps successfully attacking the center of the line, bypassing the heavily defended Futa Pass on September 1. The decisive US drive on Bologna was halted by German defenses on October 20, and it was only in December that the British 8th Army captured Ravenna.

Following a typically severe winter, the Gothic Line was effectively breached by Allied forces on April 9 and 14, 1945, supported by a massive bombing campaign. The US 10th Mountain Division forced the last mountain positions above Bologna by April 17 and broke out into the relatively flat Po Valley on April 20. Coupled with the British 8th Army forcing the Argenta Gap, the German defenses irrevocably collapsed, with the Allied armored and fully mobile mechanized infantry divisions scattering the fuel-starved and undersupplied German formations. On April 29 *Generaloberst* von Vietinghoff, who had taken over command from Kesselring, asked for an armistice, which took effect on May 2, 1945, only days before the final surrender in Europe.

***

The Italian campaign has been controversial ever since its conclusion. It was not the "soft underbelly of Europe" that Winston Churchill had predicted. The German defensive effort, largely successful despite complete Allied air supremacy, was little short of brilliant, aided by the terrain and less-than-inspired Allied leadership. The argument for the continuing Allied effort was that it tied down significant numbers of German divisions, preventing their employment on the Eastern Front and in France. However, this is only true to a limited degree, as few panzer or *Panzergrenadier* divisions, over and above those that were already in theater, were transferred to the Italian Front. It is interesting to note that apart from the last days of the campaign, the German divisions retreated in good order with most of their heavy equipment. It can be argued that Hitler gave this secondary front far less attention, thereby allowing the very experienced and extremely competent commanders there a more-or-less free hand, something that almost never happened in the East or West.

Generally, the Italian campaign did not feature large-scale clashes of armor. It was mainly an infantry battle due to the mountainous nature of the terrain. The panzer divisions were usually tightly integrated with the infantry in the defensive zones or, occasionally, held back in reserve in order to counter Allied breakthroughs. The most numerous Allied tank, the M4 Sherman, was more than matched in gun power by the 75mm L/48 of the *Panzer IV* and the *StuG III* and totally outclassed by the *Panzer V Panther* that started to appear in larger numbers in 1944. The deployment of the massive 65-ton *Sturmgeschütz mit 8.8cm PaK 43/2 "Elefant"* was a mistake, as this complex and unwieldy vehicle constantly broke down on the narrow mountain roads, where even a broken track could render it unrecoverable. Even the employment of the *Tiger I* was somewhat wasted in Italy, as it had few opportunities to utilize its long-range killing power, capable of destroying Allied armor at 3,000 meters.

ABOVE: A *Sturmgeschütz III, Ausführung G*, with supplemental armor, which possibly belonged to a tank battalion, prepares to move out somewhere in Italy. The assault gun appears to have had some time in the field, as evidenced by the rust marks and chipped paint seen on the lower hull. The top of the fighting compartment of the vehicle is covered with tarpaulins, possibly because of rainy weather and the "porous" nature of the roof, which allowed water to drip inside. The soldier standing beside the vehicle shaking hands with the vehicle commander wears the mouse-gray panzer uniform. In fact, all five of the soldiers seen in the image wear differing combinations of tanker-type uniforms, demonstrating that the Germans were not as uniform as commonly believed. (KEN NIEMAN)

FACING PAGE TOP: Large numbers of Italian *Semovente DA 75/18* assault guns were employed by the Germans in Italy and the Balkans. More than 220 were produced for the Italian forces and, after Italy's capitulation, the Germans ordered another 55. The German designation for these vehicles was *Sturmgeschütz M42 mit 7,5 KwK L 18 (850)(i)*. In this image, one of the vehicles that has been knocked out was photographed by a New Zealand soldier. Note that the vehicle is missing its rear idler wheel. The assault gun appears to have been "short-tracked," which meant that the track was run without the benefit of the idler wheel. This was a field expedient that allowed the vehicle to be moved short distances until it could be recovered by maintenance teams for repair. Stenciled in white on the left front hull is a rhomboid for a panzer unit along with an unknown emblem on the left-hand side. The latter appears to be a white circle with a vertical medieval sword, which might possibly be for the *3. Panzergrenadier-Division*. (JEFF PLOWMAN/TONY ORMANDY)

FACING PAGE BOTTOM: A Renault AHN truck parked in an Italian town sports a very "artistic" camouflage pattern. This is painted not only on the truck cab but also on the canvas bed cover. In the case of the canvas cover, it almost appears to be a three-tone camouflage pattern, given the contrast between the two paints used and the drab material of the cover itself. Also of interest is the combat-decorated NCO closest to the cab of the truck and in the foreground. He wears a custom-made M36-style tunic, possibly fabricated out of Soviet shelter-half material. (MICHAEL H. PRUETT)

A completely destroyed *Sd.Kfz. 10/5* mounts an unusual weapon: In place of the standard *2cm FlaK 38,* this vehicle was armed with the *2cm Flugabwehrkanone Scotti(i),* which was one of the two standard 2cm antiaircraft weapons employed by the Italian Army. (JEFF PLOWMAN/TONY ORMANDY)

ABOVE AND NEXT PAGE: Photographed in Italy in 1944 by a member of the US Army Air Force 317th Bomb Group, these images show a collection point for captured German vehicles. Identified in these photos: two *Sturmgeschütz III, Ausführung G*s; a *Panzerjäger 38(t) Marder III, Ausführung M*; a *Panther* from the *I./Panzer-Regiment 4*; a *Sturmpanzer IV*, commonly referred to after the war as the *Brummbär* (Grizzly Bear); and a *Ferdinand/Elefant,* vehicle *102*, from the *1./schwere Panzerjäger-Abteilung 653*. Many of these same vehicles would later be transported to the Aberdeen Proving Grounds in the United States for evaluation, where they continue to reside in the museum collection. (MICHAEL H. PRUETT)

RIGHT: The *Sturmgeschütz III, Ausführung G,* shown in the first image is seen in detail. The markings on this vehicle indicate prior service with the *2./ Panzer-Abteilung 103* of the *3. Panzergrenadier-Division.* The duplication of the white vehicle numbers on the large panel on the side of the vehicle on the commander's cupola was a typical practice of *Panzer-Abteilung 103* during its service in Italy.

ABOVE: The last image provides another view of the *Sturmpanzer IV* and the *Ferdinand/Elefant.* (Michael H. Pruett)

FACING PAGE TOP: The crew of this *Panzerjäger 38(t) Marder III, Ausführung M,* use the entranceway of an Italian building for overhead cover. The placement of reeds alongside and on the vehicle also helps in offering concealment. Three "kill rings" have been painted on the barrel of the *7.5cm PaK 40.* The driver of the vehicle, a *Gefreiter,* wears the field-gray *Sturmartillerie* uniform. His collar tabs are field-gray, piped in rose-pink, but are lacking the Death's Head devices normally seen there. (JEFF PLOWMAN/TONY ORMANDY)

FACING PAGE BOTTOM: This knocked-out *Panzer IV* may have also sought cover within the confines of some buildings, but it appears to have been of no avail.

Captured by New Zealand forces, this *15cm schweres Infanteriegeschütz 33* displays some very interesting markings and an elaborate camouflage scheme, which appears to consist of a base of *dunkelgelb* (dark yellow) with hand-painted, hard-edged splotches consisting of *rotbraun* (red-brown) and *dunkelgrün* (dark green). On the right side of the gun shield are the original German markings: the divisional emblem for the *98. Infanterie-Division*; the *13(IG) Gr. Rgt 117*, which indicates assignment to *13. (Infanterie-Geschütz)/Grenadier-Regiment 117*; and the tactical emblem for an *Infanteriegeschütz*. On the left side of the shield, the Kiwi soldiers have stenciled the nomenclature of the weapon. (JEFF PLOWMAN/TONY ORMANDY)

LEFT: New Zealand soldiers inspect captured *Panzer I* tank turrets that were intended to be employed as pillboxes. Factory modifications were made to the original turrets, such as the replacement of the machine-gun mantlet with a flat steel plate (35mm) with apertures for an *MG34* machine gun. The side-vision flaps of the original turrets were also removed and covered with steel boxes. The turrets appear to be finished in mid-war *dunkelgelb* as a base coat. Ninety-one of these pillbox turrets were sent to Italy. (JEFF PLOWMAN/ TONY ORMANDY)

A more famous use of tank turrets as field fortifications came in the form of the *Pantherstellung* (Panther position), whereby a *Panther* turret also became a pillbox. These were officially designated the *OT-Stahlunterstand mit Pantherturm*, with 56 reportedly sent to Italy in 1943 and 1944, where the mountainous terrain seemed almost ideal for this type of expedient antitank defense. The turrets themselves were modified for this purpose, with beefed-up armor protection (an additional 40mm on the roof and 70mm on the sides) and the removal of the standard commander's cupola (replaced with a hatch almost flush with the turret roof). Turret traversing was done manually, and the turret itself was placed on a prefabricated stand which was then lowered into the ground, with the lower portion serving as the crew's living quarters.

THIS PAGE: A knocked-out *Panzer V, Ausführung A,* formerly of the *I./Panzer-Regiment 4,* which was attached to the *26. Panzer-Division,* as photographed by a Kiwi soldier. At least two hits to the front of the vehicle are evident: one shot near the "letterbox" machine-gun port that did not penetrate, and another above the right drive sprocket that did. The small, square-shaped *Zimmerit* pattern is typical for a *Panther* that was manufactured by the firm of Daimler-Benz. (JEFF PLOWMAN/TONY ORMANDY)

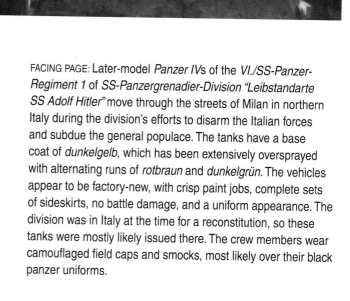

FACING PAGE: Later-model *Panzer IV*s of the *VI./SS-Panzer-Regiment 1* of *SS-Panzergrenadier-Division "Leibstandarte SS Adolf Hitler"* move through the streets of Milan in northern Italy during the division's efforts to disarm the Italian forces and subdue the general populace. The tanks have a base coat of *dunkelgelb,* which has been extensively oversprayed with alternating runs of *rotbraun* and *dunkelgrün.* The vehicles appear to be factory-new, with crisp paint jobs, complete sets of sideskirts, no battle damage, and a uniform appearance. The division was in Italy at the time for a reconstitution, so these tanks were mostly likely issued there. The crew members wear camouflaged field caps and smocks, most likely over their black panzer uniforms.

A company of factory-new *Panzer IVs* moving through the streets of a Greek city. They were most likely assigned to *Panzer-Regiment 1* of the *1. Panzer-Division*, which was sent to Greece in June 1943 in a show-of-force mission to counter the perceived threat of an Allied invasion. The crews appear to be in shirtsleeve order due to the intense summer heat. In the wake of the Italian defection from the Axis in September 1943, the division assisted in the disarming of the Italian forces in Greece.

CHAPTER 9

The Campaign in Western Europe (1944–45)

Before Allied tank crews landed in Normandy, they were assured by their superior officers that their tanks, primarily the M4 Sherman, were the equal of, and generally superior to, those of the Germans. Few of these crews had experience in directly confronting German armor, and for those men who had not experienced combat against German tanks and their battle-hardened crews, superiority was indeed believed to be the case. However, those veteran British and US tank crews of North Africa and Italy had a far less sanguine opinion. Armored clashes in Normandy soon demonstrated that these assurances were, at the very least, exaggerated.

The story of the Normandy invasion, Operation Overlord, and the subsequent campaign to break out of the bridgehead have been fully covered in large numbers of books and do not require an extensive summary here. When the Allies invaded on June 6, 1944, only the *21. Panzer-Division* was close to the invasion area. The division's main striking force was the 112 *Panzer IV*s of *Panzer-Regiment 22*; it had no *Panther*s. In the early afternoon of D-Day, a *21. Panzer-Division* counterattack actually split the Canadian "Juno" and British "Sword" beaches, but it was driven back by a combination of naval gunfire, air interdiction, and Allied reinforcements threatening to trap them. However, the division was able to stop the British drive on the strategically vital town of Caen, which was supposed to be captured on D-Day.

On June 6 alone, the Allies landed nearly 1,478 tanks and tank destroyers—1,045 British and 433 US—although many of the amphibious Duplex Drive Shermans foundered in the rough waters. Even at this early stage, the Allies enjoyed a marked superiority in armored vehicles over the Germans.

Fortunately for the Allies, there was also a disagreement between Rommel, commander of *Heeresgruppe B*, and von Rundstedt, *Oberbefehlshaber West* (commander-in-chief in the West), over the disposition of the panzer forces. Based on his experiences of crushing Allied air superiority and supremacy in Africa and Italy, Rommel wanted his armored forces close to the beaches, where they could counterattack the Allied formations immediately. Conversely, von Rundstedt wanted a centralized grouping of the panzer divisions for concentrated deployment to the invasion area.

Hitler ordered an unsatisfactory compromise: The available German armor was scattered from Belgium to Normandy, with many of the formations not available to the operational commanders except on Hitler's express order. The majority of these panzer divisions were not combat capable. They were in the process of reconstituting with new and replacement equipment and training new recruits. They seriously lacked mobility, markedly hindering their ability to move to Normandy. For instance, on June 1 the *2. SS-Panzer-Division "Das Reich"* had only some 600 motor vehicles available for use out of an authorized establishment of nearly 4,000.

Despite the delay in Hitler releasing the panzer divisions, the *II./SS-Panzer-Regiment 12* of *12. SS-Panzer-Division "Hitlerjugend,"* with its 98 *Panzer IV*s, arrived in Normandy on June 7. The battalion was immediately committed to combat, counterattacking Canadian forces to the north of Caen. The 66 *Panther*s of the *I./SS-Panzer-Regiment 12* arrived the next day, as did the 99 *Panzer IV*s of the *II./Panzer-Lehr-Regiment 130* of the *Panzer-Lehr-Division*. More *Panther*s arrived on June 10, with the *I./Panzer-Regiment 6* fielding 99. As was typical with many battalions that had just been issued the *Panther* and had conducted new-equipment training within the confines of the *Reich*, the formation saw its initial combat attached to another division (in this case, the *Panzer-Lehr-Division*). The *Tiger* finally started to appear on June 12, consisting of 45 *Tiger I*s of *schwere SS-Panzer-Abteilung 101*. Due to their lack of preparedness and transport capacity, as well as Allied air superiority, which hampered movement, the build-up of panzer and *Panzergrenadier* divisions against the Allied beachhead was understandably quite slow.

It was soon evident to Allied tank crews that the M4 Shermans and the far less common British Cromwells were not markedly superior to the most numerous German tank, the *Panzer IV*, and quite inferior to the *Tiger I* and particularly the *Panther*. The *Panzer IV* was capable of penetrating the Sherman's frontal armor at ranges of 1,000 meters and side armor at longer ranges. The Sherman could only penetrate the front turret armor of the *Panzer IV* at less than 1,000 meters but not the front hull armor. On the other hand,

it could penetrate its thinner side armor at longer ranges.

Against the *Panther* and *Tiger I*, the performance of the Sherman was another thing entirely. Even at point-blank range, the frontal armor of both the *Tiger I, Ausführung E,* and the more frequently encountered *Panther, Ausführung A or G*, could not be pierced. At very close range, the thinner side armor of the *Panther*, which was sloped, could be penetrated, but the side and rear armor of the *Tiger* was invulnerable. It is not intended to discuss the whole M4 Sherman controversy here. On the one hand, the Sherman could be considered a robust, reliable, and maneuverable tank, more than adequate for its primary mission of rapid exploitation of a breakthrough against primarily infantry forces. On the other hand, there is this account by MC Lieutenant Robert Boscawen, Troop Commander in No. 2 Squadron of the 1st Coldstream Guards, in June 1944:

> We who were serving and fighting in the American-built Shermans . . . did not hold them in high regard. Against the German Mark IV and Panther Mark V, let alone the Tiger, they were pretty useless, especially the majority [of the Shermans] which only had a 75 mm gun. They were mechanically reliable and kept going, but caught fire very readily.

The British "Firefly" version of the M4, with its excellent 17-pounder (76mm) high-velocity main gun, went a long way toward redressing the inadequacy of the 75mm gun in tank-versus-tank combat. The *Panzer IV* could be knocked out frontally at long range; even the frontal armor of the *Tiger* was vulnerable, although at considerably shorter ranges. Against the *Panther*, things were not so promising, as this account from the British 23rd Hussars of the 11th Armoured Division reveals in relation to firing trials conducted on eight *Panther*s previously knocked out from the flank:

> It was found that the 75-millimetre gun made no impression on the front at all, unless it was lucky enough to hit the turret ring, a very small target indeed. The 17-pounder was more encouraging (as related earlier,

we were equipped with one 17-pounder for every three seventy-five's) for it penetrated the front of the Panther's turret at three hundred yards. Though it did not always go through the sloped front plate of the hull. On the whole, we decided that Panthers should be treated with circumspection. In point of fact, we found ourselves in just that position a few days later, and the results were just as unhappy as our trial shoot indicated.

It should be noted that both the Tiger and Panther could knock out a Sherman at more than 2,000 meters.

Understandably, both the British and US tank crews soon developed a kind of phobia about all German tanks. The *Tiger*, in particular, developed a particularly ominous reputation. Given that that there were not more than about 126 *Tiger I*s deployed in Normandy and they were not encountered with great regularity, the widespread "sightings" of the vehicle seem hard to explain. Part of it might be explained by the superficial similarity of the smaller *Panzer IV* to the *Tiger*, particularly in stressful combat situations. Both tanks had vertical armor plates, and the curved supplemental armor around the *Panzer IV* turret was similar in appearance to the curved armor plate of the *Tiger* turret. In addition, it was more "acceptable" to be knocked out by a formidable *Tiger* than a lowly *Panzer IV*. As can be seen later in this chapter in some of the images taken by GIs, it was not uncommon to incorrectly identify knocked-out German tanks, almost always making them out to be a *Tiger*, a feat that carried considerably more weight in prestige among armored personnel.

As with the Sherman, there are conflicting opinions on the utility of the *Tiger I*: Was it an invulnerable, highly effective, tank-killing behemoth or an overweight, overrated, lumbering waste of scarce resources? As usual, the truth lies somewhere between the two extremes. Its weight of 56 tons meant that once disabled, even if the reasons were relatively trivial, it was difficult to recover, and more *Tigers* were blown up by their crews than were destroyed in combat. The introduction of the very effective *Bergepanther* (*Sd.Kfz 179*) recovery vehicle with its 40-ton winch, large spade, and 1.5-ton derrick went a long way in alleviating the problem of heavy tank recovery.

Perhaps the last word on the *Tiger I* should belong to the British Military College of Science, School of Tank Technology. In 1944 it conducted a lengthy and extensive analysis of an early-model *Tiger I* captured in Tunisia. While acknowledging its faults, the conclusion reached was as follows:

> The Pz.Kpfw. VI, with its heavy armour, dual-purpose armament and fighting ability is basically an excellent tank and, in spite of the defects noted, constitutes a considerable advance on any tank that we have tried.
>
> Its greatest weakness is probably the limit imposed on mobility owing to its weight, width and limited range of action.
>
> Taking it all round, it represents a very formidable fighting machine which should not be under-rated.

From the start of the campaign, the bulk of the German armor was concentrated against the British and Canadian divisions attempting to take Caen, rightly considered by both sides as the linchpin of the German defenses in Normandy. British and Canadian forces mounted several large-scale tank and infantry assaults against Caen with a view to capturing the city and unhinging the German Normandy defenses.

The most famous tank action of the campaign, indeed of the entire campaign in the West, took place on June 12 in response to Operation Perch. An advance group of the British 22nd Armoured Brigade of the famous 7th Armoured Division, the "Desert Rats," moved in column along the Caen–Villers-Bocage road. The division was in a position to exploit a dangerous gap between the *352. Infanterie-Division* and the *Panzer-Lehr-Division*, possibly leading to the outflanking of Caen. Notified of this incursion, *SS-Obersturmführer* Michael Wittmann of *schwere SS-Panzer-Abteilung 101* immediately commandeered *Tiger 222* and, after arranging for the other *Tigers* in the company to be alerted, proceeded to singlehandedly engage the 7th Armoured advance elements.

These advance units were A Squadron of the 4th City of London Yeomanry and part of the 1st Rifle Brigade. In rapid succession, Wittmann destroyed a Cromwell and a Sherman Firefly of A Squadron. Then, moving parallel to the column, most of the 1st Rifle Brigade's vehicles were knocked out at point-blank range. These consisted of three M3 Stuart reconnaissance tanks, fourteen M3 half-tracks, two Sherman observation/command tanks that had dummy main armament, an armored car, and at least twelve Bren and Carden-Lloyd carriers, many of these from the antitank battery. Somewhat recklessly moving into Villers-Bocage itself, Wittmann then knocked out four more Cromwells, before a 6-pounder antitank gun damaged the *Tiger*'s running gear. Wittmann and crew abandoned the tank, which was later destroyed by the British to prevent it from being recovered. By this time the remainder of the operational *Tigers* of the company had moved up to assist in blocking the British advance. By his immediate and courageous action, Wittmann had thrown the advance of an entire armored division into disarray.

A second attempt to take Caen, Operation Epsom, was launched on June 24, but it was decisively checked by German armored reinforcements and called off on July 1. On July 18 a third attempt, Operation Goodwood, which featured considerable armored strength, was once again contained, with the armored divisions suffering particularly heavy losses from tanks and antitank guns. After only modest gains, the attack was finally called off on July 20. However, nearly all the panzer and *Panzergrenadier* divisions were now concentrated in the British sector. Montgomery's subsequent contention that he never really planned for a breakthrough in this sector but was intending to fatally weaken the German armored formations in order to facilitate the eventual US breakout can be taken with several grains of salt.

In the meantime, US forces had fully consolidated Omaha and Utah beaches by June 12. They then concentrated on operations on the Cotentin Peninsula, with the intention of capturing Cherbourg, the only major port in the Normandy area. Cherbourg was duly taken on June 26, but the port facilities were thoroughly wrecked and the harbor blocked by sunken vessels as well as magnetic and acoustic sea mines. The demolitions were so effective that Cherbourg was rendered unusable for months, with the result that the ingenious Mulberry harbors along the beaches continued to be the primary landing point for supplies for some time.

On July 3 the US divisions began their slog south through the rugged *bocage* country. The thick hedgerows proved to be an invaluable aid to the German defenders and a nightmare for the attackers. Although most of the German armor was concentrated around Caen, US forces only advanced slowly and suffered considerable losses in armored vehicles to assault guns, tank destroyers, antitank guns, and handheld antitank weapons such as the *Panzerfaust* and *Panzerschreck* (the German version of the bazooka).

If the Allied tankers were disappointed by the performance of their tanks, the German troops were positively shocked by the massive firepower and material superiority of the Allies. The Germans called this type of warfare *Materialschlacht*, a war of *matériel*. The supply of tanks and other armored vehicles seemed endless, and Eastern Front veterans stated that Allied artillery strikes were heavier and more effective than anything they had encountered in Russia. In particular, Allied airpower was prodigious, with the use of four-engine heavy bombers in a tactical role devastating. Fighter-bombers continuously filled the skies, making any movement in daylight extremely hazardous.

On July 25 Bradley's US 12th Army Group broke through the German defenses in Operation Cobra. It was preceded by a massive bombing effort, with 4,000 tons of bombs dropped on the German front lines. The only German armored force at the front in that sector was the *Panzer-Lehr-Division* as well as part of the *2. SS-Panzer-Division "Das Reich."* Although some accounts indicate the former division was almost obliterated—an argument favored by airpower advocates—it was actually only seriously disrupted by the bombing. The German infantry divisions suffered severe losses, and there were no appreciable reserves. As a result, the advance of the US VII Corps was faster than expected, with Coutances taken on July 28. The mechanized and motorized US infantry easily outmaneuvered the largely foot-bound Germans.

The German left was outflanked by the US VIII Corps, which reached Avranches on July 30: The German front was collapsing. The US 3rd Army, commanded by Patton, advanced from Coutances. Showing his customary drive and mastery of armored operations, his forces were soon advancing rapidly, and by August 4 his armored spearheads had reached Mayenne. Patton was then ordered to advance on Le Mans, striking directly across the rear of the German forces. The British and Canadians were to continue to attack southward from Caen.

If things were going extremely well for the Americans, the same could not be said for the British at Caen. In support of the now-rampaging US forces in the south, Montgomery launched Operation Bluecoat from Caumont on July 31 with the XXX Corps (comprising the 43rd and 50th Infantry Divisions and the 7th Armoured Division). The corps was tasked with carrying out an encircling movement from Aunay-sur-Odon and Mont Pinçon. Progress was slow, and on August 3 a furious German counterattack was mounted, encircling the 5th Royal Tank Regiment, which had to fight its way out during the night, losing a total of seven tanks that day. The offensive petered out, with the 7th Armoured Division 8 kilometers short of its objective at Aunay-sur-Odon. Montgomery was furious at what was deemed to be a third successive failure for his "Desert Rats," and Bucknall, the commanding general of the XXX Corps; Erskine, the commander of the 7th Armoured; and more than 100 other officers were either sent back to England or reassigned to other formations.

On August 6 the Germans mounted their last large-scale counterattack in Normandy, Operation *Lüttich* (Liege), also known as the Mortain Offensive. On Hitler's express order, four understrength *Panzer* divisions—the *2. Panzer-Division*, the *116. Panzer-Division*, the *1. SS-Panzer-Division "Leibstandarte SS Adolf Hitler,"* and the *2. SS-Panzer-Division "Das Reich"*—were to break through to Avranches, cutting off the spearhead of the advancing US forces. There were not enough tanks—no more than 140 plus 30 assault guns—or fuel for the offensive to have any hope of succeeding. In addition, there was a serious lack of both infantry and artillery support, essential to a breakthrough.

Warned by Ultra intercepts, US elements were alerted and moved into blocking positions. The US 30th Infantry Division was reinforced by substantial artillery assets and augmented by Combat Command B (CCB) of the 3rd Armored Division. Although *Generalfeldmarschall* von Kluge and his staff considered the offensive a failure as early as the afternoon of August 7, Hitler wanted three *Panzer* divisions to be redeployed from the Falaise sector to reinforce the offensive. The senior German officers in Normandy knew that this would fatally weaken the defenses at Falaise, leading to the total collapse of the Normandy front.

In an effort to capture Falaise, Operation Totalize started on August 7 with almost 1,000 aircraft of RAF Bomber Command blasting the German positions. Two armored brigades and two infantry brigades attacked the *89. Infanterie-Division*, which had been shattered by the bombing and was retreating in panic. A counterattack by the *12. SS-Panzer-Division "Hitlerjugend,"* supported by 10 *Tigers* of *schwere SS-Panzer-Abteilung 101*, rallied the fleeing infantry, who returned to their positions. It was during this operation that Wittmann was killed, when his *Tiger* and two others were destroyed by a single Sherman Firefly.

The second phase of the operation involved the 1st Polish Armored Division and the 4th Canadian Armoured Division breaking through to Falaise. The German resistance was intense, and progress was slow. In one instance, a Canadian brigade-sized formation lost 50 out of 60 tanks in a clash with the *Panthers* and *Tigers* of *Kampfgruppe Wünsche*. By August 11 "Totalize" was over, with the Canadian II Corps having advanced 15 kilometers, although the corps was still 12 kilometers short of Falaise. The encirclement of the *7. Armee* and the *5. Panzer-Armee* was nearly complete, however, and time was running out for a successful withdrawal.

Patton was very close to securely closing the gap with 21st Army Group, but he was halted by Bradley outside of Argentan in order to avoid any possible disastrous accidental clash with Montgomery's forces. This delay, although understandable in the confused circumstances, indirectly led to large parts of the German forces escaping the pocket. Allied airpower and long-range artillery was turning the retreat into a rout, as von Kluge appealed to Jodl to convince Hitler to approve a withdrawal from central and southern France. The German general withdrawal began on August 16, although some battered units had been sent east earlier and *Generalfeldmarschall* Model had now taken over command from von Kluge. The panzer divisions fought valiantly and mostly successfully to hold the remaining narrow escape route open.

The pocket was closed on the evening of August 19, but the perimeter was thinly held in places. Many German units continued to break out, aided by a counterattack of the *II. SS-Panzer korps*—only able to muster 15 tanks and 3 battalions of infantry—the next day. The scene inside the pocket was one of complete chaos, with thousands of trucks and staff vehicles destroyed, although relatively few armored vehicles. About 40,000 German prisoners were taken, but another 40,000 troops and some of their heavy equipment escaped the pocket to fight another day. The main blame for the failure to trap all the German forces has been placed with the 1st Canadian Army failing to reach Falaise fast enough and in sufficient strength. Its two armored divisions, the 4th Canadian and 1st Polish, were inexperienced formations and this was their first major battle, begging the question: Why were these two divisions the spearhead of the assault rather than more experienced armored formations?

With Allied forces in furious pursuit, German forces crossed the Seine by ferries and pontoon bridges in the last days of August, managing to extricate considerable numbers of men, armor, and vehicles. Paris was liberated on August 25 against very little opposition, and the vital port of Antwerp captured on September 3. It seemed that the entire German Army in the West was in complete disarray, and there were no appreciable armored forces available for counterattacks. Total defeat in a relatively short period of time seemed inevitable, but somehow the Germans, with their improvisational skills, managed to cobble together ad hoc units out of the stragglers and hastily incorporated reinforcements. The *Westwall* (Siegfried Line) was manned along the border of Germany in early September. German efforts were aided by the Allies now operating at the end of long supply lines. Antwerp not able to be used for unloading supplies and troops until late November.

Montgomery initiated an uncharacteristically daring and risky plan to drive into Germany and capture the vital industrial area of the Ruhr. Code-named Operation Market Garden, three airborne divisions—two US and one British—were to seize vital bridges over the Rhine in Holland, with the powerful British XXX Corps of Horrocks leading the assault. Although most of the bridges were captured, the last and most vital bridge at Arnhem remained in German hands. The *9. SS-Panzer-Division "Hohenstaufen"* and the *10. SS-Panzer-Division "Frundsberg"* happened to be in Arnhem at the time, although they were very much understrength and in the process of reconstitution. Both divisions had almost no tanks, but they were subsequently reinforced with an assortment of *Panzer IV, Panther, StuG III, Jagdpanzer IV, Tiger I*, and, late in the battle, *Königstiger* tanks.

The British armored units were unable to break through to the surrounded British 1st Airborne Division, as the German defenses were now too strong. On September 25 the paratroopers were ordered to break out and attempt to reach British lines, with very few managing to do so. On September 26 "Market Garden" was called off. Against determined opposition, the Allies continued to advance slowly but inexorably. They were confident, despite the temporary setback, that the end of the war was only a matter of a few months away. However, the resilient Germans had one more surprise to spring.

On December 16, 1944, the "quiet" sector of the Ardennes exploded as nearly 1,900 guns and rocket launchers unleashed a furious barrage on four resting US divisions of General Middleton's VIII Corps. The initial attack on a 130-kilometer front was spearheaded by 5 panzer and 13 infantry divisions, with 200,000 men and 600 tanks and assault guns. The 4 US divisions had 83,000 men, 242 tanks (mainly M4s), 182 tank destroyers, and 392 artillery pieces. Although the attackers initially had significant numerical superiority, the resources the Allies could eventually bring to the battle were overwhelming.

The attack took the Allies by complete surprise. With their overdependence on Ultra intercepts, little notice had been taken of front-line intelligence assessments and information from prisoners. To add to the confusion, there was Operation *Greif*, commanded by Otto Skorzeny, with English-speaking German soldiers in US uniforms and captured vehicles, including *Panther*s cleverly disguised as M10 tank destroyers. Although their material effect was marginal, the havoc they created behind Allied lines was considerable, with widespread confusion and suspicion. Even senior US officers, including Bradley, were required to answer sometimes-obscure questions from guards at checkpoints that only "real" Americans could answer.

The spearhead of the *6. Panzer-Armee* was the *1. SS-Panzer-Division "Leibstandarte SS Adolf Hitler"* with 34 *Panzer IV*s, 38 *Panzer V*s, and 21 *Panzer IV/70(V)*s. *Kampfgruppe Peiper* was to lead its assault, with around 90 tanks, including about 35 *Panzer IV*s, 35 *Panther*s, and some 20 *Königstigers* of *Schwere SS-Panzer-Abteilung 501*. For the *5. Panzer-Armee*, the resolute *2. Panzer-Division* led the assault with its 28 *Panzer IV*s, 59 *Panzer V*s, and 47 *StuG III*s. Even though the panzer divisions were brought up to nearly full strength in terms of personnel, tanks, and assault guns, they were desperately short of all types of staff vehicles, trucks, and prime movers. Even more critically, there was a shortage of fuel. Instead of five times the basic allowance deemed necessary for combat operations, only one and a half times was delivered, and most of the ammunition supplies were still on the east bank of the Rhine and unable to get to the front-line units.

Although the early days of the offensive approximated the heady days of the May 1940 *Blitzkrieg*, with some opposing forces being swept aside, others defended stoutly, disrupting the already ambitious German assault timetable. This was particularly true in the sector of the US V Corps, which stubbornly defended the important Berg-Bütgenbach-Elsenborn area on the northern shoulder of the advance. On December 17 the US 7th Armored Division was deployed to hold the vital road junction at St. Vith and the US 101st Airborne Division to reinforce the equally important junction at Bastogne. Unable to capture Bastogne in the initial assault, the Germans bypassed the town, leading to significant difficulties in both maneuver and supplying the advancing formations.

Two divisions of the VIII Corps, the 4th Infantry Division and 9th Armored Division, checked the attack of the *7. Armee*. After only a small advance by the Germans, the southern shoulder of the salient was now firmly held by US forces. On the right flank, *Kampfgruppe Peiper*'s ruthless advance was held up at Stoumont, and by December 19 it was both desperately short of fuel and well ahead of the rest of the *6. Panzer-Armee*. The advance of that field army was disappointing and von Rundstedt recommended reinforcing the advance of the *5. Panzer-Armee*, but Hitler refused.

On December 19 Allied higher headquarters finally recognized the scope of the German attack and immediately rushed 60,000 troops to the threatened front, with another 180,000 arriving over the next eight days. Making things worse for the Germans, the skies cleared on December 23 and the bombers and fighter-bombers were out in force. In a remarkable maneuver, Patton redeployed the II Corps of his 3rd Army and relieved the beleaguered defenders of Bastogne on December 26. Two days earlier, *Kampfgruppe Peiper*, out of fuel and ammunition, abandoned all its heavy weapons and retreated from partially surrounded positions on foot. To the south, Manteuffel's forces finally forced the 7th Armored Division and 106th Infantry Division out of St. Vith, but by then this was too late to have any effect on the advance. The defeat of the *2. Panzer-Division* at Celle on December 26, with part of the division encircled, effectively signaled the end of the German advance.

On December 28 the US 12th Army Group counterattacked, and Hitler agreed that a withdrawal to the *Westwall* position was necessary. Montgomery's 21st Army Group began its counterattack on January 3, 1945.

At its deepest, the attack had gained some 115 kilometers and caused considerable Allied, mainly US, casualties of some 80,000 killed, wounded, and taken prisoner, with some 800 armored vehicles destroyed or captured. On the German side, total casualties were also around 80,000, with approximately 600 armored vehicles destroyed or captured. The US units fought both bravely and with considerable skill, and their supposedly inferior tanks and tank destroyers knocked out considerable numbers of the vaunted panzer force.

The elimination of the "bulge" was not accomplished until January 16, with the Germans slowly pushed back to their original positions. The stubborn defense of the salient was, according to Manteuffel, responsible for more casualties than the original assault. The German armored forces in the West almost ceased to exist, as the majority of the remaining panzer divisions were transferred to the collapsing Eastern Front. The Ardennes offensive caused the Allied drive on Germany to be delayed by about six weeks.

Against 3 weak German Army Groups (H, B, and G), with only 26 understrength divisions and very weak in armored vehicles, Eisenhower's forces consisted of 85 full-strength divisions, with 23 of them armored and 5 airborne. In terms of tanks and assault guns, the Germans fielded perhaps 250 on the entire Western Front against 3,500 medium and light tanks of the US 1st and 9th Armies alone. The total Allied tank and tank destroyer inventory was more than 16,000.

In the final assault into Germany, the US 1st Army unexpectedly seized a slightly damaged but serviceable bridge over the Rhine at Remagen on March 7 and established a small bridgehead from which it started its drive into Germany on March 25. The British and Canadians, along with the US 9th Army, crossed the lower Rhine on March 23, as did Patton's 7th Army and the French 1st Army.

The US 1st and 9th Armies surrounded the remnants of Model's *Heeresgruppe B* in the "Ruhr Pocket" on April 1, with 317,000 German troops surrendering on April 18. The Allied and Soviet armies on both fronts were advancing up to 80 kilometers a day as resistance collapsed. On April 11 9th Army spearheads reached the Elbe River. They halted there, since this was the agreed-upon demarcation line between Allied and Soviet forces. The British Army reached the Elbe on April 24, taking Hamburg on May 3. The Germans surrendered unconditionally to Allied forces on May 7, to take effect the next day. The Soviets, for their part, accepted the surrender in Berlin on May 9. The war in Europe was finally over after six cruel and incredibly destructive years.

NEXT TWO PAGES: This series of images comes from a scout assigned to *SS-Panzer-Aufklärungs-Abteilung 1 "Leibstandarte SS Adolf Hitler"* and were possibly taken shortly before the invasion of Normandy in June 1944 or in the early fall when the formation was being reconstituted.

FACING PAGE TOP LEFT: The first photograph shows two comrades during a break in activities. Interesting from a uniform perspective, the scout on the viewer's right wears a relatively rare variant of the panzer uniform, a reed-green herringbone-twill version that was made for the *Waffen-SS*. These were originally designed for crews of armored reconnaissance vehicles because the traditional black uniform stood out too much when the crews dismounted to perform duties. Although regulations stipulated that insignia were not to be worn on the uniform, the scouts of the battalion did not adhere to this requirement, as can be seen here and in the next two images.

FACING PAGE TOP RIGHT: The scout discussed in the previous image with other comrades of his section.

FAACING PAGE BOTTOM: This scout also wears the reed-green uniform as he poses on the back deck of an *Sd.Kfz. 233*. The camouflage seen in the image was probably applied in the field, given the extensive overspray seen on the vehicle's tires.

ABOVE LEFT AND RIGHT: Two views of an *Sd.Kfz. 251/9* (early version with the offset 75mm main gun), a vehicle not often photographed.

ABOVE LEFT AND RIGHT: Two views of an *Sd.Kfz. 250/10*, which was the vehicle earmarked for platoon leaders of reconnaissance platoons and featured a 37mm *PaK 35/36* mounted on the front of the superstructure. This modification was done as early as the French campaign in 1940, but these are later variants of the vehicle.

"Ursula," a *Panzer V, Ausführung A,* of the *I./Panzer-Regiment 6,* which had been attached to the *Panzer-Lehr-Division,* was knocked out during the fight for La Caplainerie near Le Désert on or about July 11, 1944. A young GI from one of the combat commands of the US 3rd Armored Division poses in front of the vehicle. It was common in the *I./Panzer-Regiment 6* to christen vehicles with the names of wives or sweethearts. These names were usually painted on the front of the travel lock mount, as seen here. The 1st Battalion was detached from the *6. Panzer-Division* in late 1943 so that it could be reconstituted and reorganized in the West with the *Panther.* In early 1944 it was attached to the *Panzer-Lehr-Division,* temporarily being redesignated as the *I./Panzer-Regiment 130* during the fighting in Normandy, until it rejoined its parent regiment and division in August 1944, when it reverted to its original designation. This type of "floating" attachment for the battalions being reequipped with the *Panther* was quite common, with some of the battalions remaining with their "temporary" divisions of attachment until the end of the war, thus causing even more confusion in associating units with particular divisions. (MICHAEL H. PRUETT)

Two additional views of *"Ursula."* In these photographs, the tank is seen being inspected by US 3rd Armored Division personnel. This tank, along with two other *Panther*s, was knocked out by flank shots fired by M10 tank destroyers of the 3rd Platoon, Company A, 899th Tank Destroyer Battalion, in the early morning hours of July 11, 1944. This vehicle was a very popular attraction for US Signal Corps photographers and GIs passing through the area, as this engagement was one of the first actions where US forces had encountered the *Panther*. It has appeared in many other postwar publications, usually with the charred remains of two crewmen strewn across the engine deck. By the time these 3rd Armored Division troops arrived on the scene, the remains had been removed from the vehicle.

The *Panzer-Lehr-Division* suffered a serious setback from this operation. The marshy terrain and thick *bocage* seriously hampered the deployment of the German armor. *Panzer-Lehr-Division* losses amounted to 10 *Panther*s from the *I./Panzer-Regiment 6* and 8 *Panzer IV*s from the *II./Panzer-Lehr-Regiment 130.* The Flamethrower Platoon (*Flammpanzerzug*) from *Panzergrenadier-Lehr-Regiment 902* and the bulk of the *I./Panzergrenadier-Lehr-Regiment 901* were either destroyed or captured. (MICHAEL H. PRUETT)

ABOVE LEFT: This *Panther*, also assigned to the *I./ Panzer-Regiment 6*, was also knocked out by M10 tank destroyers during the fight for La Caplainerie. The vehicle, christened *"Elna,"* is an early-model "hybrid" *Ausführung A*. On this version the chassis remained identical to the earlier *Ausführung D,* but it had the new improved turret of the *Ausführung A* installed.

ABOVE RIGHT: In the image with the GI posing on the main gun, a large hole can be observed at the top juncture of the right frontal plate and side armor (below the GI's feet). This shot was apparently a "lucky strike" in that the penetration could have been the result of a defective weld seam. A second round has pierced the front fender and, judging from the angle of the hole, possibly penetrated the hull side above the track.

LEFT: A final view of *"Elna,"* this time viewed from the rear. This vehicle had a spare roadwheel mounted on the engine deck and a *Balkenkreuz* painted between the exhaust pipes. Judging from the location of the house on the right, *"Elna"* was probably following right behind *"Ursula"* when it was knocked out. (MICHAEL H. PRUETT)

TOP: This GI, a member of the Anti-Tank Company of the 39th Infantry Regiment of the 9th Infantry Division, strikes a pose in front of a *Panzer V, Ausführung A,* of the *I./Panzer-Regiment 6,* which was destroyed during the fighting near Le Désert.

BOTTOM: In the next image, other GIs of the company are seen inspecting the burned-out remains of another *Panther*, also an *Ausführung A.*

More knocked-out *Panther*s from the engagement near Le Désert. In the top image, the left storage sponson box has been knocked off or removed from the vehicle and one of its spare roadwheels lies next to it along the roadside embankment. The bottom *Panther* seems to have suffered more catastrophic damage inasmuch as the torsion bars for the roadwheels appear to have broken, allowing the chassis to "sink," causing the idler wheel and the drive sprocket to appear to almost touch the ground.

LEFT: This *Panzer V, Ausführung A*, from the engagement near Le Désert shows evidence of having burned out. Souvenir hunters or scavengers also appeared to have thoroughly gone through the vehicle, as demonstrated by the opened stowage and sponson boxes.

BELOW: A final view of a knocked-out *Panther* from the *Panzer-Lehr-Division* near Le Désert. Souvenir-hungry GIs have looted the rear stowage bins of this *Panther*. The crew's clothing, papers, and personal affects litter the ground behind the vehicle. (MICHAEL H. PRUETT)

TOP: Personnel of Combat Command B of the US 3rd Armored Division inspect a *Panzer V, Ausführung A*, of the *I./SS-Panzer-Regiment 2* destroyed on the road near Coutances in Normandy on July 30, 1944. The field-expedient camouflage placed in front of the vehicle would indicate that this *Panther* was lying in ambush, covering any movement coming down the road. One hit can be detected on the gun mantlet that deflected down into the radio operator's compartment. The vehicle is completely burned out. The *Zimmerit* has burned away from the vehicle's turret and sides, and the rubber on the roadwheels has been reduced to ashes.

BOTTOM: In the second image, the three GIs are amused by an article of clothing found in the vehicle's stowage bin. A panzer crewman's "trophy" has now become a souvenir of the GIs. (MICHAEL H. PRUETT)

TOP: Abandoned in a French farmyard, this *Panzer IV* is possibly from the *V./Panzer-Lehr-Regiment 130,* since the small white turret numerals are hallmarks of some of the companies of that battalion (other companies used red numerals outlined in white). A GI inspects the inside of the turret from the loader's hatch, while a truckload of soldiers passes. Of note here is the missing right track. Its absence is hard to explain, unless the crew removed it with another vehicle prior to its abandonment in an effort to make it inoperable. Additional track has been placed along the front slope of the vehicle to enhance armor protection for the crew.

BOTTOM: In the next image, *Panzer IV* number *545* sits along the roadside. It may have burned out from the inside, as evidenced by some of the discoloration to the paint job on the hull and turret. Marked in white chalk above the engine air intake louvers is the word *checked*, with what appears to be a date below. This indicates that American troops have inspected the vehicle for mines or booby traps. (MICHAEL H. PRUETT)

LEFT: A GI poses for the camera aboard a captured *Sd.Kfz. 251/9, Ausführung D,* also referred to as the *Stummel* (Stump). This is the earlier version of the vehicle, with the main gun offset to the right on the upper superstructure. The later versions had the main gun mounted higher and centrally on the front of the fighting compartment. This vehicle has no unit markings, but the *WH* (*Wehrmacht Heer* = Armed Forces – Army) on the license plate painted on the front hull indicates this vehicle probably belonged to an army *Panzergrenadier* or *Panzer-aufklärer* element. It is very likely that it belonged to the *Panzer-Lehr-Division,* as photographs of other half-tracks of this division have a *WH-15* sequence license plate.

RIGHT: In the second image, a small-caliber penetration—perhaps a sub-caliber, high-velocity round or a British 6-pounder (57mm)—of the gun's front protective plate can be observed. In the background is a destroyed *Panzer IV* with a large *05* painted on the rear of the turret sideskirts, indicating perhaps a company headquarters vehicle of the 5th Company of the *Panzer-Lehr-Regiment.* (MICHAEL H. PRUETT)

An *Sd.Kfz. 162 Jagdpanzer IV, Ausführung F*, is abandoned on a street in the town of Châteaudun, near Orléans, France. This vehicle has a uniform coat of *Zimmerit* and is painted in dark yellow with splotches of red-brown and olive-green paint. This *Jagdpanzer IV* belonged to the 2nd Company of an unknown *Panzerjäger-Abteilung* and has a red-painted numeral, *212*, outlined in white. Three divisions that fought in Normandy were issued the *Jagdpanzer IV*: the *Panzer-Lehr-Division*, the *9. SS-Panzer-Division "Hohenstaufen,"* and the *12. SS-Panzer-Division "Hitlerjugend."* The second image was obviously taken some time later, as evidenced by the additional debris left by scavengers around the vehicle and the opened window shutters. (MICHAEL H. PRUETT)

This *Panzer V, Ausführung A*, photographed near St. Lô, is being inspected by curious GIs. Of interest are the three metal grab handles welded to the front slope of the tank near the radio operator's hatch. These have been added to assist the crew in mounting the vehicle. This vehicle may have been issued to *SS-Panzer-Regiment 2*, since the *2. SS-Panzer-Division "Das Reich"* participated in the engagements that took place around the city. The tank may have been abandoned, as there are no obvious signs of battle damage. (MICHAEL H. PRUETT)

This *Sturmgeschütz 40, Ausführung G,* the last production series of the venerable *Sturmgeschütz III*, was destroyed at the side of a building in France. It has a waffle-pattern application of *Zimmerit*, and no vehicle numbers have been applied. An internal explosion has completely blown the roof off the vehicle, a not uncommon occurrence in assault guns, when the onboard ammunition detonated in a sympathetic explosion. In tanks, this frequently resulted in the turret being dislodged or completely blown off the vehicle. (MICHAEL H. PRUETT)

This press-release image was captioned: "New tanks roll to the front in the West." In it, two 18-ton *Famo* prime movers are positioned in front of a stationary *Panzer V, Ausführung D,* which is being passed by another one. The *Famo* vehicles may be there to assist or recover the *Panther,* which might have broken down. Note the full-length coveralls worn by the crew of the first *Panther* in line. The photograph is dated October 21, 1944. (KEN NIEMAN)

These *Panzer IVs* of *Panzer-Abteilung 115* of the *15. Panzergrenadier-Division* were completely destroyed during the fight for Geilenkirchen near Aachen, Germany. The close proximity of the vehicles and the extent of their damage indicate they may have been caught by surprise, perhaps by an air strike. The *Panzer IV* on the viewer's right is an *Ausführung J*, while the middle tank is an *Ausführung H*. The variant of the left-hand vehicle cannot be ascertained. The rear of the right-hand *Panzer IV* displays the divisional emblem, a three-pointed star. Certain sources have stated that this marking was only used while the division served in Italy. This photograph discounts that theory. (MICHAEL H. PRUETT)

This *Panzer V, Ausführung G*, believed to have served with the *II./Panzer-Lehr Regiment 130*, is seen beside a ruined house in Alsace in the fall of 1944. The numeral *535*, painted in red and outlined in white, appears on the turret sides. At this time, the battalion consisted of two companies of *Panther*s (5th and 7th) and two companies (6th and 8th) with *Panzer IV*s. The crew has applied hasty camouflage to the vehicle using debris taken from the building, indicating it probably only anticipated being in the area for a short while. (KEN NIEMAN)

FACING PGE: Knocked out near Martelange, Belgium, during the Ardennes offensive, this *Sd.Kfz. 142/2 Sturmhaubitze 42* lies abandoned in a stream. This "light Nazi tank" as written on the edges of the original photograph, displays some very interesting features. Three markings can be seen on the rear hull: a standard *Balkenkreuz*; an unknown unit marking, which appears to be a black diving eagle holding a shell in its talons, painted on a shield; and, next to this, the vehicle number *311* in white. On the vehicle's fighting compartment sides, a framework has been added that has been fabricated from angle iron and pipe. Attached to the framework are metal 7.92cm ammunition cans. The main gun is missing its muzzle brake, and the short appearance of the barrel is possibly due to its being out of battery. This image, and a number to follow, were all taken by a US medic. (MICHAEL H. PRUETT)

LEFT: While serving near Wiltz in Luxembourg, the GI medic took this photograph of a destroyed *Panzer V, Ausführung G*. This "King Tiger" appears to have burned out, based on the blackening seen on certain parts of the hull and turret as well as the large amounts of *Zimmerit* that have flaked off on the front slope. The misidentification of tanks was common among all soldiers of all armies during the period, with a "King Tiger" possibly sounding more menacing than a "Panther." (MICHAEL H. PRUETT)

Three American tank officers survey a completely burned-out *Panzer V, Ausführung G.* Note that the officer on the left wears his M1 steel helmet over his leather tanker's helmet. This photograph is captioned on the back: "Jerry tank captured during the Ardennes breakthrough, December, 1944." (MICHAEL H. PRUETT)

FACING PAGE TOP: It is believed this photograph was taken after the abortive attempt of *Kampfgruppe Kuhlmann*—a battle group composed of almost all of the armored elements of the *12. SS-Panzer-Division "Hitlerjugend"* and the attached *schwere Panzerjäger-Abteilung 560*—to take Dom Bütgenbach during the opening stages of the 1944 Ardennes offensive. This *Jagdpanther* was knocked out at the edge of a tree line. It lacks any vehicle numbers and has a camouflage paint job that appears to have been hastily applied. The heavy antitank battalion probably only had one company of *Jagdpanther* tank destroyers. It was one of the best tank destroyers of the war, and nearly 415 of all variants were produced at three different manufacturing facilities. Its 88mm main gun was the same as that mounted on the *Königstiger*. As with most late-war German armor, it was a case of "too little and too late" for it to make a difference. (MICHAEL H. PRUETT)

FACING PAGE BOTTOM: The *III./SS-Panzergrenadier-Regiment 26*, attached to *Kampfgruppe Kuhlmann* for the operation, lost a number of its *Schützenpanzerwagen* (*SPW*)—armored personnel carriers—during this engagement. Photographed not too far from the *Jagdpanther* seen previously is this *Sd.Kfz. 251, Ausführung D*, which has suffered a direct hit from either artillery or tank fire, being completely destroyed in the process. Since a main-gun round would normally penetrate right through the thin armor of a half-track, the death blow most likely came from artillery fire. The GI who took this photograph shot a number of views of this *SPW* and its fallen crewmen, but the images are far too graphic for this study. The only markings on this half-track are a *Balkenkreuz* painted on the sides. The license plate panel painted on the front plate has had the *SS* runes omitted as well. (MICHAEL H. PRUETT)

TOP: Photographed during the Ardennes fighting, an American 2nd lieutenant proudly poses atop a burned-out *Panzer V, Ausführung G*. Painted in overall dark yellow, this *Panther* has an interesting camouflage pattern. Patches of green paint have been sprayed on, which were then outlined in red-brown.

BOTTOM: In the second image, another service member poses astride the main gun and the cause of the vehicle's demise is clearly seen: A penetration caused the 7.5cm ammunition to ignite, blowing a large hole in the side hull armor. Note that the muzzle brake is missing from the main gun, giving an interesting view of the threaded end of the gun barrel. As with many instances where there was a sympathetic explosion from the onboard ammunition, the torsion bars appear to have been shattered as well, causing the "sunken" appearance of the tank. (MICHAEL H. PRUETT)

TOP: A *15cm schwere Feldhaubitze 13/1 (Selbstfahrlafette) auf Geschützwagen Lorraine Schlepper (f)* is seen abandoned beside a road in northwest Europe during the winter of 1944–45. Depending on the source, 160 of the vehicles were fabricated, marrying the 15cm field howitzer with the chassis of the captured French Lorraine 37L tracked prime mover. The German-modified vehicles were primarily deployed in North Africa and the West. Painted in overall dark yellow, this vehicle also has an application of dark green as camouflage. It features a large *Balkenkreuz* and a white-outlined red numeral *622* (tactical number). Since the 6th Battery of *Panzer-Artillerie-Regiment 155* of the *21. Panzer-Division (neu)* was issued these self-propelled guns, this vehicle may have been from that unit. (MICHAEL H. PRUETT)

BOTTOM: In this image, another use of the *Lorraine Schlepper* can be seen, this time the *7.5cm PaK 40/1 Geschützwagen Lorraine Schlepper (f) "Marder I"* during some sort of training exercise. Only 170 were built by a field command in France known as *Baukommando Becker*. This vehicle has the emblem of the *15. Infanterie-Division*, which was reconstituted in France in 1942 but which also makes the vehicle somewhat of a mystery, since no source lists that division's antitank battalion—*Panzerjäger-Abteilung 15*—as having received this particular tank destroyer.

ABOVE: This US M4 Sherman, probably a late-production M4A2 based on the additional side armor, was captured intact by the *5. Fallschirmjäger-Division* in Wiltz and employed in its service. The vehicle was extensively marked with the *Balkenkreuz* and is seen in January 1945, abandoned beside the Hôtel des Ardennes in Esch-sur-Sûre. Apparently the GIs found a new use for this vehicle after it was returned to them: Notice the "One Way" sign mounted next to the right headlight guard. (MICHAEL H. PRUETT)

FACING PAGE: Two very interesting views of an abandoned *Panzerkampfwagen Tiger, Ausführung B*—usually referred to as the *Königstiger,* King Tiger, Royal Tiger, or *Tiger II*—which had been assigned to the headquarters of *schwere Panzer-Abteilung 506. Tiger 03* was abandoned near Villers la Bonne during the Ardennes offensive. The battalion, which had been formed in May 1943, had fought on the Eastern Front until August 1944, when it was ordered out of the line and returned to Ohrdruf for reconstitution and reorganization with the *Königstiger.* In all, the battalion had 47 *Tiger* tanks when it started the offensive on December 21, although its 4th Company was composed of the *Tiger I.* By the end of the offensive, which saw little combat employment of the tanks due to the rough terrain of the Ardennes, the battalion was reduced to 30 operational tanks. (MICHAEL H. PRUETT)

ABOVE: This destroyed *Panzerfeldhaubitze 18M auf Geschützwagen III/IV (Sf) Hummel, Sd.Kfz. 165*, commonly referred to as the *Hummel* (Bumblebee), was photographed by a member of the US 6th Armored Division in 1945. It has a three-color "ambush"-style camouflage paint job consisting of large circles of green and red-brown applied over the dark yellow base coat. Originally designed in late 1942, the *Hummel* saw service from 1943 until the end of the war within the self-propelled battalions of the divisional artillery of armored and mechanized divisions. By the end of the war, more than 700 vehicles had been produced, with an additional 150 ammunition carriers also fabricated. (KEN NIEMAN)

FACING PAGE: This *Panzer V, Ausführung A*, is believed to have belonged to the *II./Panzer-Regiment 33 "Prinz Eugen"* of the *9. Panzer-Division* and destroyed during the street fighting in Cologne, Germany, in early March 1945. Although the vehicle took numerous hits on the frontal armor, of which none appear to have penetrated, one round has succeeded in blowing off the driver's visor. The GIs seated on the turret wear the triangular patch of the US 3rd Armored Division on their left shoulders. (MICHAEL H. PRUETT)

FACING PAGE TOP: American troops inspect a knocked-out *Sd.Kfz. 7/2 2cm Flakvierling*. One of the vehicle's former crew members has drawn a cartoon of a cat about to pounce on a bird on the inside of the gun. (MICHAEL H. PRUETT)

FACING PAGE BOTTOM: In this image, the same type of vehicle stages an "engagement mode" for the photographer. The "exposed" positioning of vehicles like this was used to trick enemy aircraft into attacking, only to find out too late what was on board the vehicle. Of interest is the limbered ammo trailer and the *SS* license plates. Normally the ammunition trailer would be positioned at some distance from the vehicle to prevent collateral damage in the event of a strafing attack by aircraft and the resultant sympathetic explosion of stored ammunition. The crew appear to be wearing *SS* camo smocks. The ammunition carrier and possibly the half-track are painted in a three-tone camouflage color with a base coat of dark yellow (*dunkelgelb*) and splotches of red-brown (*rotbraun*) and olive green (*olivgrün*).

BELOW: Sherman tanks of the US 2nd Armored Division pass an abandoned *15 cm Panzerwerfer 42 auf Selbstfahrlafette, Sd.Kfz. 4/1*, near Elze, Germany, in the spring of 1945. Possibly the victim of a mechanical breakdown, this *Panzerwerfer* is painted in overall dark yellow. Approximately 300 units were produced from March 1943 until the end of the war. The 10 15cm rockets were capable of being fired in salvo or individually. While not as accurate as artillery, the barrage fire from these rockets generally produced greater psychological effects when employed properly. No attempt has been made to further camouflage the vehicle beyond the factory finish of overall dark yellow. (MICHAEL H. PRUETT)

FACING PAGE: American GIs pose beside a knocked-out *Tiger I*, date and place unknown, although presumably along the abortive Seine crossing site at Rouen for the German forces at the end of the Normandy campaign. The narrow white-outlined numeral *141* painted on the turret would suggest that this vehicle formerly served with the *1./schwere SS-Panzer-Abteilung 102*. This vehicle has a coat of *Zimmerit* and a three-color camouflage paint job, typical of the *Tiger I*s of this formation. By September 1, 1944, the battalion had lost all of its tanks during the fighting in Normandy and the crossing of the Seine. It was reconstituted, reorganized, and redesignated at Camp Senne in Germany in the fall of 1944, before it was sent east, where it fought on the Eastern Front until the end of the war as *schwere SS-Panzer-Abteilung 502*, equipped with the *Tiger II*. (MICHAEL H. PRUETT)

LEFT: *Jagdpanther 123* of *Kampfgruppe Paffrath* (*schwere Panzerjäger-Abteilung 654*) received numerous hits while engaging American M36 tank destroyers near Kaimig-Ginsterhain on March 13, 1945. A GI took a close-up photograph of the damage inflicted on the vehicle.

BELOW: An image widely circulated on the internet (without attribution), which shows the same vehicle next to a knocked-out M36. Close inspection of both images shows that the *123* was probably assigned to another company of the battalion at some point in time, since there are vestiges of another numeral, largely covered with camouflage paint, farther to the rear of the fighting compartment. (MICHAEL H. PRUETT)

A US Army Air Corps officer poses beside an abandoned *Königstiger* somewhere in Germany. Note that the main gun is locked in full recoil, possibly indicating that the crew disabled it after a mechanical breakdown. Further evidence of this is demonstrated by the engine grille on the ground next to the tank and the removed bow machine gun. Typical of late-war German vehicles, this *Tiger II* lacks the application of vehicle numbers or unit insignia. Only a small *Balkenkreuz* has been painted on the turret. Despite the lack of unit-identifying features, the vehicle appears to have had a carefully applied three-tone camouflage scheme. Some of the mudguards are missing; whether this is the result of rough field handling or scrap-metal scavengers is not known. (MICHAEL H. PRUETT)

Two knocked-out combat vehicles at Waldhof, Germany, in 1945: a late-model *Panzer V, Ausführung G*, and a late-version *Sturmgeschütz III, Ausführung G*. The assault gun's black-painted *323* appears beside a small *Balkenkreuz*. The *Panther* was at one time equipped with infrared night-fighting devices, as the special armored stowage box for the *FG1250* auxiliary equipment is mounted. The *FG1250* was a 200-watt screened light used in conjunction with the infrared receiver/gunsight. Together, the range was 600 meters at night in clear weather. Although the Germans were well advanced in the development of night-vision devices, their employment on the battlefield was limited and sporadic. The *Panther* also sports an interesting camouflage scheme, which appears to be the familiar tricolor pattern painted over the primer coat of red oxide, but with portions of the latter remaining exposed to create a four-color effect. In addition, it had the "chin"-type gun mantlet, which was designed to eliminate the potential shot trap of the fully rounded mantlet. (MICHAEL H. PRUETT)

ABOVE: Judging from the number of spent shell casings piled on the engine deck, this late-version *Sturmgeschütz III, Ausführung G*, put up quite a fight before finally being knocked out. This vehicle is fitted with the roof-mounted remote control for the machine gun. (KEN NIEMAN)

RIGHT: Photographed sitting on the floor at the Skoda factory in Pilsen, Czechoslovakia, are roof-mounted remote-control machine-gun devices. Notice that the mount in the center has inventory control numbers stenciled to the mounting column. This photograph has also been rotated 360 degrees to provide the viewer with better detail. (MICHAEL H. PRUETT)

TOP: An abandoned *Sd.Kfz. 2 Kleines Kettenkraftrad HK 101*, or *Kettenkrad*, displays the red-and-white unit emblem of *Sturmgeschütz-Brigade 667* painted on the front mudguard. By the end of the war, more than 8,000 of the vehicles had been produced, seeing service on all fronts from 1941 on. It was popular in the units and was used in a variety of roles, where a rugged cross-country vehicle was needed. Indeed, the nimble vehicle continued to be produced after the war as an agricultural tractor, with production finally ceasing in 1948–49. Although the parent brigade saw action primarily on the Eastern Front, the formation was returned to Germany in late 1944 and reconstituted. From then on, it fought in the West. (KEN NIEMAN)

BOTTOM: In the second image, most likely taken along the Eastern Front in late 1944, a *Kettenkrad* negotiates muddy terrain with a *Sonder-Anhänger 1* in tow, which appears to be stringing wire for field telephones. The soldier standing in the back of the vehicle carries a *Sturmgewehr 44*, the world's first assault rifle, which allowed selective fire from a 30-round magazine and had an effective range out to 300 meters in semiautomatic mode.

This *Panzer V, Ausführung G*, was often photographed shortly after the end of the war. According to MacDougall and Block, it was one of the last *Panther*s, if not the last *Panther*, to have been completed by the firm of MAN and delivered to German forces in April 1945. It is believed to have been issued to the *I./Panzer-Regiment 3* and captured by US forces near Salzburg, Austria, before being transported to its famous location on the *Karlsplatz* in downtown Munich. These photographs were taken by the US medic whose images of destroyed German armor are found elsewhere in this book. (MICHAEL H. PRUETT)

CHAPTER 10

The Campaign in Eastern Europe (1944–45)

From December 24, 1943, to early 1944, a series of operations was mounted along a 900-mile front. Designated "Right Bank Ukraine," it had the intention of destroying both *Heeresgruppe A* and *Heeresgruppe Süd*. From April 8 to May 12, 1944, alone, there were 10 separate operations—11 if the Crimean operation is counted—employing five fronts with 2,000,000 troops, 4,000 tanks and assault guns, and 4,000 aircraft.

Hitler, as usual, interfered in the conduct of the defense with his habitual no-retreat orders, producing the inevitable disastrous effects, like the trapping of 60,000 to 70,000 men in the Korsun-Tscherkassy Pocket. Manstein, mindful of Stalingrad, dispatched a relief force that included eight panzer divisions to free the encircled four infantry divisions, the *5. SS-Panzer-Division "Wiking,"* and other formations. On February 15 Hitler finally gave the garrison the order to break out, achieving a linkup with the *III. Panzer korps* on February 18. A total of 36,000 men were claimed to have broken out, leaving all their heavy equipment behind, but two experienced corps were effectively destroyed and played no further part in the fighting. The German relief forces suffered more than 20,000 casualties and heavy tank losses, while Soviet losses were estimated at 80,000 men and 700 tanks.

The 1st Ukrainian Front broke through to Tarnopol and Proskuroz, separating the *1. Panzer-Armee* and the *4. Panzer-Armee*, while the 2nd Ukrainian Front shattered the *8. Armee*. A massive gap was created between *Heeresgruppe A* and *Heeresgruppe Süd*. The offensive continued without letup. Not even the spring thaw slowed the Red Army down, leading to a separation of the increasingly nervous German forces in Poland from those in southern Russia. By April 17 the Soviet offensive had progressed unabated for four months, advancing from 250 to 500 kilometers to the Polish border and the Carpathian Mountains, eliminating the entire southern sector of the German forces. From April 8 to May 9, the Red Army retook the Crimea in an operation of stunning rapidity, shattering the *17. Armee* in the process, inflicting more than 100,000 casualties. In the north, another major operation relieved the besieged Leningrad by January 20, the German forces being pushed back more than 150 kilometers in places into Estonia.

Generaloberst Schörner took over command of *Heeresgruppe Südukraine*, formerly *Heeresgruppe A*, and *Generalfeldmarschall* Model now commanded *Heeresgruppe Nordukraine*. The previous commanders in chief, Kleist and Manstein, had fallen out of Hitler's favor. In the case of Manstein, the best operational-level general in the German Army was now permanently removed from command. If the situation looked remorselessly grim to the Germans in April, it was to become far worse in June.

***

The Red Army was no longer just quantitatively superior in armor, but it was rapidly catching up in the quality of its tanks as well. The T34/85, with its high-velocity 85mm main gun housed in a redesigned three-man turret, was intended to counter the *Panther*, now considered its most dangerous opponent at the front. A tank battalion in mid-1944 consisted of 21 T34/85s, three of these battalions forming the principal striking force of a tank brigade. Although the new T34 was not quite a match for the *Panther*, it was markedly superior to the *Panzer IV, Ausführung J.*

Also appearing at this time was the formidable IS-2 "Stalin," with its heavy armor and massive 122mm D-25T main gun. The IS-2 gave both the *Tiger I* and the *Panther* plenty of headaches, as it was capable of destroying either vehicle at normal combat ranges of 1,000 meters. However, both German tanks could also knock out the "Stalin" at that range, and their superior optics gave them an edge at long ranges. The "Stalin" also only carried 28 rounds of main-gun ammunition, limiting its effectiveness in sustained combat situations.

In addition, there were new tank destroyers, such as the SU-85/100; light infantry support vehicles, such as the SU-76; and heavy assault guns, such as the SU-122/152 and ISU-122/152 (firing massive shells of 25 and 49 kilograms, respectively). All of these vehicles were manufactured in substantial numbers, with some 4,500 of the ISU-122/152 being produced. The supply of 450,000 US-built jeeps and, more importantly, the exceptional 4×4 and 6×6 trucks ensured that the supply lines functioned smoothly.

On the German side, the latest versions of the *Panther*, the *Ausführung A* and *Ausführung G*, had finally reached an acceptable level of reliability, and the new armored vehicles like the *Jagdpanther*, with its superb 88mm L/71 main gun, and the massive *Panzer VI, Ausführung B "Königstiger,"* mounting a similar weapon, were all powerful vehicles but produced in far too few numbers to have any significant effect on the course of the war.

The role of the panzer and *Panzergrenadier* divisions had now fundamentally changed. They were employed as "fire brigades," sent either to threatened parts of the front or where the Red Army mobile forces, usually tank armies, had broken through. Every effort was also being made to ensure that artillery and antitank guns were mounted on fully tracked chassis, as towed weapons were now becoming extremely vulnerable to the devastating Soviet artillery barrages. Despite the large-scale bombing effort in Europe by the US and British air forces, armaments production was increasing at a rapid rate, but this could not continue for long, as the German resource base continued to shrink. Increasingly, the armored and mobile units suffered from gasoline, ammunition, spare parts, and other essential supply shortages, severely hampering their operational flexibility.

***

Until the middle of 1944, *Heeresgruppe Mitte* had defeated all previous Red Army attempts to advance, and the front lines had barely changed since late 1943. It was expected that a renewed Soviet offensive would occur in the south, and this assessment was reinforced by a brilliant deception plan (*maskirovka*) on the part of the Soviets that convinced the German high command that this was indeed the case. Of the 30 panzer and *Panzergrenadier* divisions at the front, 24 were concentrated in the south.

Operation Bagration commenced on June 22, exactly three years after the commencement of Operation Barbarossa. The Red Army committed 19 combined-arms and 2 tank armies, composed of 1,400,000 men, more than 5,000 tanks and assault guns, and 31,000 field pieces and heavy mortars against *Heeresgruppe Mitte* alone. Those field armies had the support of more than 5,000 aircraft. The primary aim was not so much to liberate territory but to completely destroy *Heeresgruppe Mitte*, with its 1,200,000 men, 900 tanks and assault guns, and 9,500 pieces of artillery. *Luftwaffe* support amounted to around 1,300 aircraft, with perhaps 50 percent of them operational.

The German troop dispositions could almost be characterized as suicidal, with large and virtually immobile garrisons stationed, at Hitler's insistence, in the "fortress cities" of Bobruisk, Mogilev, Orsha, and Vitebsk. These groups positively invited encirclement and subsequent destruction. This occurred without achieving any slowing down, let alone the defeating, of the Soviet offensive. So overwhelming and rapid was the Soviet offensive that the panzer divisions in the south were almost powerless to intervene as *Heeresgruppe Mitte* quickly collapsed, its demise hastened by Hitler's customary no-retreat orders. By the end of August, as the Soviet offensive finally wound down, the German field-army group had ceased to exist as an effective force, suffering an estimated 300,000 killed, wounded, and missing—a disaster greater than Stalingrad and Germany's greatest defeat of the war. The Red Army reached the border of Prussia in the north, and in the south were only 100 kilometers from Warsaw.

From July to November 1944, the Red Army advanced through the Baltic states, isolating the *16. Armee* and *18. Armee* of *Heeresgruppe Nord*, with their 33 divisions, in the Courland Peninsula. The *Kriegsmarine* was able to evacuate substantial numbers of men and *matériel*, but 21 divisions—189,000 troops—remained in *Heeresgruppe Kurland*, as it was redesignated on January 26, 1945. This grouping was subjected to repeated, intensive attempts by the Soviets to liquidate the pocket. However, these attacks were all defeated, inflicting huge casualties on the Red Army, and the garrison did not finally surrender until May 9, 1945.

Although the Germans had fortified the front between the Vistula and Oder with seven defensive zones some 300 miles deep, they had neither the troops to fully man them nor the artillery and antitank guns to reinforce them. The whole German defensive structure in the East was falling apart. The Soviet forces were far too strong, and their commanders were now highly skilled at directing mobile operations. In stark contrast, German generals were continually hamstrung by Hitler's increasingly inane orders to hold at all costs. Ground down by the massive Allied round-the-clock air offensive over Europe, the *Luftwaffe* could no longer provide even minimal air support. The apparent success of the few German armored counterattacks was illusory and, in the long run, achieved nothing.

Warsaw, or what was left of it after the failed Polish Home Army uprising, fell on January 17, 1945, as German commanders disobeyed Hitler's order to hold and wisely withdrew. In a brilliant encircling maneuver by the Soviets, the vital Silesian industrial region was captured intact. After a 500-kilometer advance in two weeks, the 1st Byelorussian Front had established several bridgeheads across the last river obstacle before Berlin, the Oder, only some 60 kilometers from the city.

In the extreme south, the Romanian front, which had been calm for four months, suddenly exploded on August 20. The 2nd and 3rd Ukrainian Fronts attacked Frießner's *Heeresgruppe Südukraine* and trapped 18 German divisions of the *6. Armee*, as well as the Romanian 3rd Army. On August 23 Romania switched sides and declared war on Germany. On September 8 Soviet forces crossed the Bulgarian border, with Bulgaria also declaring war on Germany the next day. The remnants of *Heeresgruppe Südukraine*, renamed *Heeresgruppe Süd*, and Wöhler's understrength *8. Armee* were pushed back into Hungary.

As the Red Army pushed into Hungary, it suffered one of its few significant late-war setbacks. The Debrecen Operation (October 6 to 28) was initiated with the intention of Malivivski's 2nd Ukrainian Front destroying Frießner's *Heeresgruppe Süd*. This led to a number of large armored engagements from October 10 to 28.

The commander in chief of the *6. Armee*, *General der Artillerie* Fretter-Pico, ordered his *1. Panzer-Division* and the *13. Panzer-Division* to encircle and destroy Group Pliyev's advancing III Corps, consisting of the 4th and 5th Cavalry Divisions and the 23rd Tank Division. The *23. Panzer-Division* and *Panzergrenadier-Division "Feldherrnhalle"* were to act as reinforcements and flank protection. By October 12 trapped Soviet elements broke out of the thinly held encirclement, and Group Pliyev was able to capture Debrecen on October 20. Rather than moving back to defensive positions, Frießner was convinced by his chief of staff, *Generalmajor* Grolman, to counterattack instead. While Wöhler's *8. Armee* took the Soviet forces in the flank, Fretter-Pico's main forces—the *1. Panzer-Division* and the *23. Panzer-Division*, spearheaded by *schwere Panzer-Abteilung 503* and its *Königstiger* tanks—attacked eastward once again, trapping Group Pliyev. The western arm of Frießner's attack consisted of the *3. Gebigsjäger-Division*, the *15. Gebigsjäger-Division*, and the *8. SS-Kavallerie-Division "Florian Geyer,"* with its 30 to 40 *StuG III*s and *Jagdpanzer 38(t)*s.

This time, there was no breakout, and relief efforts by Malinovsky's forces were decisively defeated in a veritable storm of artillery and particularly effective tank and antitank gunfire, inflicting significant tank losses. By October 29 the trapped formations destroyed their heavy weapons and broke out on foot. Group Pliyev suffered some 25,000 casualties in killed, wounded, and missing, along with 360 tanks and more than 1,000 artillery pieces, antitank guns, and heavy mortars captured or destroyed. This was the last successful large-scale German counterattack on the Eastern Front.

For the Soviets, however, this was only a temporary setback, as the operations to take Budapest were launched on October 29. By December 26, after particularly heavy fighting, Budapest was surrounded. Six divisions were trapped—two armored (*"Feldherrnhalle"* and the 13th), two Hungarian infantry (10th and 22nd), and two *SS* cavalry (8th and 22nd)—plus a miscellany of infantry and other armored units. In all, about 70,000 personnel were surrounded, of which approximately 55 percent were Hungarian. Despite three relief attempts—*Konrad I*, *Konrad II*, and *Konrad III*—featuring strong *SS* and army armored units, the Soviet defensive ring was too formidable to be broken, despite exceptional efforts by the German units. The desperate defenders of Budapest could not hold out for long against the overwhelmingly superior Red Army forces, and the city finally fell on February 13, most of it totally destroyed.

The Soviet forces reached Lake Balaton on March 5, and Hitler ordered a counteroffensive called *Frühlingserwachen* (Spring Awakening). The *6. SS-Panzer-Armee* attacked from north of the lake and the *2. Panzer-Armee* from the south against Tolbukhin's 3rd Ukrainian Front. Despite initial success, an advance of 32 kilometers in the first 24 hours, the attack slowed to a crawl due to a combination of the muddy spring conditions and Tolbukin's hastily prepared defensive positions, some up to 45 kilometers deep. Nevertheless, the brutal fighting continued unabated for 10 days, with both sides suffering considerable tank and personnel casualties, before the Germans, after coming within 24 kilometers of Budapest, broke off the offensive on March 15, conserving what was left of their armor for the final defense of the rapidly diminishing *Reich*. By April 4 the 3rd Ukrainian Front was within 8 kilometers of Vienna, and by the 13th had taken total control of the city.

By April 10 only a total of 2,200 German tanks and assault guns were available for combat operations along the entire Eastern Front. Most of these were *StuG III/IV*s and *Jagdpanzer 38(t)*s.

For the Berlin operation, Zhukov's 1st Belorussian Front, Rokossovsky's 2nd Belorussian Front, and Konev's 1st Ukrainian Front consisted of 2,500,000 troops, 6,250 tanks and assault guns, and 45,000 artillery pieces and rocket launchers. These were supported by 7,500 aircraft. *Heeresgruppe Weichsel* and *Heeresgruppe Mitte*, the main opposing forces, deployed 770,000 troops, including the Berlin garrison, which consisted mainly of boys of the Hitler Youth and old men of the *Volkssturm*. They were supported by 1,500 tanks and assault guns, with the *Luftwaffe* somehow scraping together about 500 operational aircraft, mainly fighters.

Against such overpowering numbers, the issue was never in doubt. The divisions manning the commanding Seelow Heights offered stiff resistance, with the main armored opposition coming from the *Panther*s of *Panzer-Division "Müncheberg"* along with the *Königstiger* tanks of *schwere Panzer-Abteilung 512*. The heavy *FlaK* batteries that had relocated from Berlin also took a heavy toll on Soviet armor, with even the IS-2 "Stalin" formations suffering harsh losses. The Seelow Heights took two days to break through, from April 16 to 17. After surprisingly stubborn German opposition, it was only on April 26 that 500,000 troops, supported by 12,700 artillery pieces, 2,000 rocket launchers, and 1,500 tanks and assault guns, attacked the city center. Despite their overwhelming superiority, the Red Army suffered heavy infantry and armored vehicle casualties in the vicious street fighting, with the final fighting for the symbolic *Reichstag* lasting from April 30 to May 2. On May 2 the commander of the Berlin garrison, *General der Artillerie* Weidling, surrendered the city. Just like Berlin, the Third Reich was now shattered almost beyond recognition.

A paratrooper poses on the barrel of a *Panzer V, Ausführung D*, somewhere in the Soviet Union. Based on the three-color camouflage scheme seen on the *Panther*, the image was most likely taken sometime in late 1943 or later. Both the vehicle and the soldier are veterans: The *Panther* shows evidence of hard campaigning, and the *Fallschirmjäger*—identified by his paratrooper badge—is also a recipient of the Iron Cross, First Class, and the German Cross in Gold. The turret marking of *A13* is unusual, with the *A* possibly indicating the *Panther* was assigned to a battalion headquarters.

FACING PAGE: A *Waffen-SS* gunner on a *Flakvierling 38* mounted on an *Sd.Kfz. 10/4* half-track scans the skies for signs of enemy aircraft, while an assistant gunner maintains vigilance along the ground. The gunners wear the *SS* camouflage smock and the *SS*-cut overseas cap. The back of the vehicle is loaded with equipment and personal items. Although this crew belonged to an unidentified *Waffen-SS* element, army shelter halves are used to cover portions of the gun platform. This may be a posed image, since none of the rest of the crew is seen—notice the four gas-mask containers—although the remainder may be resting or carrying out other duties while "air guard" duty is performed.

BELOW: The whitewash applied to this *Sd.Kfz. 10/4* and *FlaK 38* has worn almost completely off, even though it appears that winter is still in full force. Since the whitewash was usually applied using field-expedient methods, it did not take much wear and tear or precipitation to remove it. Of interest are the mounting of the hand grenades along the front shield of the gun as well as the "kill" marks indicating the shooting down of at least three aircraft and the destruction of other unidentified targets.

A later-model *Panzer IV*, possibly an *Ausführung G*, sports a relatively intact coat of whitewash and has had *Winterketten* (winter tracks) mounted to its running gear. The crew stays bundled up in the frigid conditions, especially since there were no personnel heaters on armored fighting vehicles. The crew has placed additional stores and two roadwheels on the front slope of the tank, added "insurance" against the harsh conditions of winter in the Soviet Union. The vehicle is probably not too close to the front, since the muzzle covers are still in place on the main gun and the coaxial machine gun.

TOP: Several *Panzer V, Ausführung G*s move by rail at an unknown location. Given their overall muddy condition, they may be close to the front or coming from some training area within Germany or occupied areas. The main gun has a muzzle cover, and there is a plug on the machine-gun ball mount to help prevent dirt and debris from entering the vehicle. Railway transportation of tracked tactical assets remained of vital importance to the Germans to avoid wear and tear on their already overtaxed fleets. Unit histories are full of descriptions of rail movements for distances as short as 50 kilometers.

BOTTOM: In the second image, a *Waffen-SS* mechanized unit prepares to move by rail. The *Sd.Kfz. 251*s have been given a coat of whitewash. Bales of hay line the station platform. These were often used to provide makeshift bedding and rudimentary insulation in the unheated railcars the soldiers frequently had to travel in.

ABOVE: Germans in the field were never averse to impressing captured Soviet equipment into service against its former owners. This was especially true of the T34 series of tanks, where entire units were equipped with them. By early 1944 the T34/76 was ending its service life. Its immediate replacement, the T34/85, started being fielded in February 1944. Armed with the more powerful 85mm main gun and newly designed turret, it was also used by the Germans, whenever one was captured. Both T34s show signs of battle damage: The one in the foreground uses a cable to keep the driver's compartment hatch open and has had a portion of its main-gun mantlet chipped out by some sort of antitank-gun fire, while the one behind it may not even be operational due to the penetration mark in the middle of the left side of its turret.

FACING PAGE: This late-model *Panzer IV* makes use of natural foliage and a tree line to provide itself with a great deal of concealment from the ground and the air. The latter was especially important in the second half of the war, when the Germans no longer enjoyed air parity, let alone air superiority or air supremacy, especially in the West.

FACING PAGE TOP: The commander of a heavily camouflaged *Panther* observes the terrain to his front, possibly checking out the twin columns of smoke on the horizon or looking for any signs of enemy activity. Given his exposed stance and lack of headphones, he probably does not anticipate any immediate combat activity.

FACING PAGE BOTTOM: This later-model *Panzer IV* appears to have had some sort of multicolor camouflage applied to its hull and turret sideskirts, but the tank itself retains its basic, factory-applied dark yellow finish, which also features a coat of *Zimmerit* on the vertical planes of the vehicle's surface. Although the time period is well after the middle of 1943, the crewman continues to wear the black version of the M34 enlisted field cap, which had been officially replaced, first by the M42 cap and then, in 1943, with the M43 field cap.

BELOW: Despite the increasing mechanization of all field armies in World War II, traditional trench warfare was not unheard of, especially on the Eastern Front. In this case, late-model *Panzer IV*s in the background provide cover along a trench line somewhere in the East.

As the war progressed, efforts to improve armor, armament, and mobility increased exponentially for both the Axis and the Allies. The Germans introduced any number of new and/or improved weapons systems, but most were a question of "too little and too late." Two designs that met with some success and saw considerable employment in 1944 and 1945 were the *Jagdpanzer 38 (Sd. Kfz. 138/2)*, frequently referred to as the *Hetzer* ("Pursuer" or "Hunter"), and the *Jagdpanzer IV/Panzer IV/70*, both based on the existing mechanically sound chassis of the *Panzer 38(t)* and the *Panzer IV*. Armed with a 75mm L/48 main gun, the *Hetzer* was issued primarily to the antitank battalion of infantry divisions, starting in the summer of 1944. In all, more than 2,500 were produced by war's end, and the Czech firm of Skoda continued producing the vehicle after the war for both the Czech and Swiss armies.

Despite the large numbers produced, photographs of the vehicle in use in the field are relatively rare. In this image, an early version of the tank destroyer moves down a crowded city street with most of its crew riding outside the vehicle, enjoying the mild weather. A *Panzer V, Ausführung G*, is parked along the thoroughfare, showing signs of extensive field use. Of interest is the large number of spare track placed along the sides and rear of the turret in an effort to increase the survivability of the tank and crew.

Rarely photographed in a field setting, this is a Vomag version of the *Panzer IV/70(V)*. In all, there were three major variants of the *Jagdpanzer IV/Panzer IV/70* family of vehicles (not counting the prototype series), each featuring a long-barreled 75mm main gun. The production version of the *Jagdpanzer IV* had a main gun of 48 calibers (*PaK 39*), with 769 manufactured between January and November 1944. This was followed by two other versions, which featured different main guns of even more caliber length. These were redesignated as the *Panzer IV/70*, with one being built by Vomag (August 1944 to April 1945) and the other by Alkett (August 1944 to March 1945). Both featured a modified *PaK 42* as a main gun, with the former featuring a very low silhouette and the latter a boxier fighting compartment. Vomag produced 930 vehicles; Alkett, 277. Although an effective tank destroyer, Guderian was against the project, since he felt it diverted from the production of the *Panzer IV* and, moreover, the *Sturmgeschütz III* was adequate for this task. As was often the case, however, Hitler personally intervened and ordered full development of the series.

In this image, a tanker poses in front of his vehicle, wearing reed-green herringbone-twill trousers designed for crews of armored fighting vehicles along with his traditional blank panzer tunic and M43 standard field cap. Of interest is the placement of a round in a vertical position on the roof of the fighting compartment.

FACING PAGE: An unidentified *Nebelwerfer* unit appears to be conducting some sort of training behind the lines in the Soviet Union or Eastern Europe. Given the condition of the *28/32cm Nebelwerfer 41* rocket launchers and the *Sd.Kfz. 10/1* prime movers, it would appear the unit has just deployed to the East or received new equipment and personnel there. As its name implies, the launcher was capable of firing two differently sized rockets, with the 28cm high-explosive rocket weighing 82kg and carrying a payload of 50kg. The 32cm rocket was filled with 50 liters of incendiary oil, which was capable of covering 200 square meters. As an area-fire weapon, it was not particularly accurate, but it did not need to be to achieve its effect.

An *Sd.Kfz. 250/1* from an armored reconnaissance battalion—possibly from a *Waffen-SS* element, based on the decals on the helmets of two of the dismounted soldiers—moves back through a village during what appears to be a retrograde operation. Some of the buildings have been set alight, with the right-hand dismounted soldier carrying what appears to be a man-pack flamethrower, the *Flammenwerfer 41*. During withdrawal operations, it was common for both sides to torch built-up areas to deny the enemy the use of infrastructure, particularly during winter months. The *Sd.Kfz. 250* seen here is the "old" version, which featured a more elaborately constructed superstructure. This later gave way to the "new" version, introduced in late 1943, which featured streamlined construction. The light half-track proved to be successful, with more than 6,500 manufactured from 1940 to 1945 in about 12 variants, not counting specially modified ones produced as forward observer (*Sd.Kfz. 253*) and ammunition carrier (*Sd.Kfz. 252*) versions.

TOP: In this image, a section of *Sd.Kfz. 250/1 (alt)* half-tracks from an armored reconnaissance battalion prepare for operations. Although the location and date are unknown, the headgear and the weather indicate the image was taken no earlier than late 1943. The vehicles appear to be painted in a base coat of dark gray to which splotches of dark yellow have been applied.

BOTTOM: A column of light reconnaissance half-tracks moves down a village street somewhere in the Soviet Union.

FACING PAGE TOP: This *Sd.Kfz. 250/1 (alt)* from a company headquarters section appears to have had a three-tone camouflage scheme applied. A tarpaulin has been placed over the rear half of the open fighting compartment, probably in an effort to protect the crew from the elements and to allow map work to be performed under dry conditions. Both the tactical numerals and the *Balkenkreuz* appear to be in outline form, with the former in red or black and the latter in white.

In this image taken in the Soviet Union in September 1943, late-model *Panzer IV*s line up in preparation to support an operation, while infantry assemble in the foreground. By this stage of the war, the German Army was well prepared to deal with an Eastern winter and camouflage overgarments such as these were a common sight. The *Panzer IV*s have had a coat of whitewash applied over their factory-applied base coat of dark yellow. Other than the *Balkenkreuz,* no other identifying marks can be seen. Several sideskirts are missing from the lead tank, probably victims of rough handling in the field.

Produced by three different firms—FAMO, MAN, and Daimler-Benz—the *Marder II* was one of several tank destroyers pressed into service following the shock of the widespread introduction of the T34 and KV1 in 1941 and 1942. The "Marten" used a *Panzer II* chassis and mounted a 75mm *PaK 40* as its main gun in a lightly armored superstructure. In all, more than 650 of the vehicles were produced from June 1942 to early 1944 and issued primarily to the antitank battalions of panzer and *Panzergrenadier* divisions. When used properly—in a "shoot and scoot" mode—the tank destroyer was highly effective. In this image, a battery of *Marder IIs* passes dismounted infantry in a muddy field, sometime in 1943.

A *Volkswagen Typ 166 Schwimmwagen* in the service of a reconnaissance element of *SS-Panzergrenadier-Division "Das Reich."* Although the army also used the vehicles, they are primarily associated with the *Waffen-SS*. Fielded in late 1942, more than 14,000 of the four-wheel-drive amphibious vehicles were produced by war's end, making it the most-manufactured amphibious vehicle in history. Given the large number of water obstacles in Europe and European Russia, amphibious vehicles were a logical development for reconnaissance forces. The soldiers wear the popular camouflage smocks, as well as billed field caps also made out of camouflage material.

RIGHT: Despite the miserable conditions, these soldiers of the *1. SS-Panzer-Division "Leibstandarte SS Adolf Hitler"* appear to be taking everything in stride. Based on the faded whitewash finishes on the *Schwimmwagen* and the staff vehicle in the background, as well as the very muddy conditions and the lack of foliage on the trees, this image was probably taken in the spring of 1944, perhaps during the efforts to relieve the Tscherkassy Pocket.

BELOW: A *Schwimmwagen* carries a machine-gun section across a body of water. The *MG34* is mounted on a tripod, allowing it to be removed rapidly from the vehicle during combat operations.

The soldiers wear camouflage smocks and covers for their helmets. In addition, the vehicle itself has had some natural vegetation and foliage added to aid in camouflaging it.

TOP: This *Tiger II* with a Henschel production turret was photographed in Bohemia in late 1944, perhaps at a training area. It appears almost factory-new and features a three-color hard-edged camouflage scheme in the so-called ambush pattern, which consisted of contrasting colors being randomly painted in small blotches over the base colors. Interestingly, the barrel has not been camouflaged and might have retained a red-oxide primer coat from the factory. Note also that the hull machine gun does not appear to have been mounted.

BOTTOM: This *Panzer V, Ausführung D*, was photographed somewhere on the Eastern Front in 1944. Since production of the *D* model of the *Panther* ceased in September 1943 and this tank looks practically new, it might be a vehicle that had undergone factory refit or overhaul and reissued to the front. The *Panther* appears to have a three-tone camouflage pattern and a complete set of basic-issue items, as well as at least one spare roadwheel and numerous sections of spare track.

FACING PAGE TOP: A *Stumgeschütz III* supports infantry during an attack. Apparently there is no threat of artillery fire or antitank gun fire, since the soldiers are bunched up around the vehicle or using the rear deck for cover. The assault gun appears to have had considerable front-line service, as indicated by the muddy appearance of the running gear and sideskirts and the well-worn whitewash finish, which has been rubbed off in places. The only identifying marks appear to be the small *Balkenkreuze* on the sides, rear, and possibly front of the vehicle. The *Stumgeschütz III* continued to have a vital front-line role until the end of the war.

FACING PAGE BOTTOM: This assault gun follows infantry in snow flurries. As with most armored vehicles, the rear deck and, to a lesser extent, the sides served as a collection point for personal items and equipment that could not be conveniently stowed inside the fighting compartment of the vehicle.

LEFT: Maintenance and repair of tanks in the field is a never-ending task. In this image, mechanics and tankers work on the suspension of *Panther 424* from an unknown battalion. The track has been "broken" to replace damaged links or give access to the suspension for other repairs. One soldier uses a "tanker bar" to help restore a portion of the front mudguard to its former position. A portion of the track remains on the drive sprocket to allow the driver to move the track on the ground back onto the suspension. From a uniform perspective, the image is interesting because most of the soldiers wear the work uniform associated with armored vehicle crewmen and mechanics, which was fashioned out of a dark blue herringbone-twill denim material.

Panzergrenadier set up hasty defensive positions next to a tank or assault gun. The *Sd.Kfz. 251s* appear to be staging prior to moving off to set up in offset positions to give the dismounted soldiers covering fire. Proper positioning of the half-tracks was critical, particularly in a hasty defense, since they needed to be close enough to provide effective fire support while, at the same time, far enough away so as not to draw additional fire on the exposed infantry. Of course, the armored vehicle is in clear violation of this rule, suggesting that this might be a training exercise.

In this image, scouts are seen moving into defensive positions that appear to be more prepared than in the previous photograph. The lead soldier is about to walk on a roofed-over enclosure, which suggests either a sleeping bunker or possibly a dug-in fighting position. Note the top of a ladder on the viewer's right, which leads into the ground. The uniforms seen represent a blend of the old and the new, with the lead soldier, a decorated *Unteroffizier*, who is armed with an *MP44*, wearing a M36 or M40 field blouse with a pair of winter overgarments, which were developed in response to the harsh conditions of winter in the Soviet Union. The soldier on the viewer's right wears a complete camouflage (and reversible) winter overgarment.

FACING PAGE TOP: Employed as a "fire brigade" on the Eastern Front, *Panzergrenadier-Division "Großdeutschland,"* like its *Waffen-SS* counterparts, was sent to hot spots. Unlike many army formations, which were regionally based in peacetime, *"Großdeutschland"* accepted soldiers from all parts of the *Reich* to fill its ranks. Well-equipped and trained, it was considered an elite formation. These *Panzergrenadier* are instantly recognizable because of the distinctive insignia identifying them as being assigned to the division: a *GD* monogram on their shoulder straps and a cuff title with the word *Großdeutschland* (Greater Germany) embroidered on it in *Sütterlin* script, an old-fashioned German writing style. The two soldiers both carry the *Panzerfaust*, a handheld single-shot rocket-propelled grenade that was introduced in late 1943. The initial version, the *Panzerfaust 30*, had an effective range of only 30 meters, but it could penetrate up to 200mm of armor, making it a very deadly weapon in close-quarters fighting. The weapon was used until the end of the war, and it was the direct predecessor to a number of successful postwar designs.

FACING PAGE BOTTOM: An early version of the *Sd.Kfz. 251/9, Ausführung C*, moves at speed down an unimproved Soviet road. The vehicle was most likely assigned to one of the two *Panzergrenadier* regiments of *Panzergrenadier-Division "Großdeutschland,"* as can be seen by the division's insignia, a white helmet outlined in black. Both of these images were probably taken in East Prussia in late 1944.

BELOW: Two half-tracks—an *Sd.Kfz. 250/5 (alt)* command vehicle and an *Sd.Kfz. 251, Ausführung D*—move down a muddy unimproved road in Lithuania in July 1944. These vehicles belonged to *Kampfgruppe Schmidt* (led by the commander of *Panzer-Regiment 11* of the *6. Panzer-Division, Oberst* Schmidt, and formed from the *II./Panzer-Regiment 11* [*Panzer IV*] tanks); *I./Panzer-Regiment "Großdeutschland"* (*Panther*s commanded by Austrian Knight's Cross recipient *Major* Walter Pössl); and other elements from the *6. Panzer-Division*. Of particular interest is the emblem painted on the front of these vehicles, a variation marking for the *6. Panzer-Division*. This emblem consisted of a white shield with a black downward-pointing arrow with red "wings" extending from it. The emblem has previously been misidentified in a number of publications as belonging to the *20. Panzer-Division*. This photograph was originally part of the photo archive of *Ersatz-Brigade "Großdeutschland."*

ABOVE: A column of *Panzer V, Ausführung G*s is halted along a road, allowing this soldier the opportunity to pose for a photo. Based on the soldier's camouflage trousers, this is most likely an *SS* unit. The *Panther*s feature a coating of *Zimmerit* and a slowly eroding coat of camouflage whitewash. (KEN NIEMAN)

FACING PAGE TOP: Soldiers march along a roadside ditch as two *Panther*s move along the unimproved roadway. The camouflage appears to be a three-tone pattern, featuring diagonally slanting alternating colors. Although the tanks appear to be relatively new, the trail *Panther* has already lost a portion of its sideskirts. These *Panther*s have the "chin"-type mantlet, which was introduced in September 1944, although *Panther*s with rounded mantlets continued to be produced until war's end.

FACING PAGE BOTTOM: A platoon of whitewashed *Panzer V, Ausführung G*s provide cover for German soldiers moving to the rear. Generally, armored or mechanized forces were tasked with performing rearguard duties, since dismounted elements had no chance of pulling back once Soviet forces had established contact.

An *Sd.Kfz. 11* towing a limbered *leichte Feldhaubitze 18* moves at speed down a dusty, unimproved road somewhere in the southern Soviet Union. Based on the tactical sign and the insignia, this gun is from the divisional artillery of the *5. SS-Panzer-Division "Wiking."*

A late-model *Panzer IV* leads an *Sd.Kfz. 251/1 II, Ausführung D*, past the ruins of a farmstead somewhere in the Soviet Union. Several of the sideskirts on the *Panzer IV* are in danger of being dislodged completely and falling off.

Armored combat engineers wait to depart a railhead with their *Sd.Kfz. 251/7s*. The half-tracks, which appear to be factory-new, are painted in a base coat of dark yellow with a camouflage pattern in olive green.

CHAPTER 11

Supporting the War Effort (1939–45)

Scouts assigned to the reconnaissance battalion of the *7. Panzer-Division*, *Kradschützen-Bataillon 7*, enjoy nice weather while being transported by rail somewhere in France in 1942. The division had been pulled out of the line along the Eastern Front and was sent to occupied France to conduct a reconstitution. While there, it was earmarked to participate in Operation *Lila*, which was intended to keep the Vichy French from scuttling their fleet at Toulon.

Launched on November 27, 1942, Operation *Lila* succeeded in keeping the French fleet from escaping Toulon and joining the Allies in North Africa, but it failed to stop the French from scuttling most of their fleet, including all of their important flagships and ships of the line. This later-model *Panzer IV* of the *II./Panzer-Regiment 25* sits on the quay next to a scuttled French battleship. Despite the reconstitution of the division and its issuance of many new items of equipment, this tank has seen considerable previous use, as evidenced by the rusting and heat marks on its exhaust system. It appears that more than 30 20-liter fuel cans have been placed on the vehicle to extend its operating radius for the long distances covered during the operation. An aerial recognition panel has been placed on top of them to avoid any friendly fire incidents.

A new *Panzer V, Ausführung G, Panther* moves at speed down a tank trail, possibly at the Grafenwöhr Training Area. The vehicle appears to have a two-tone camo scheme, with a base color of dark yellow and an overspray of perhaps olive green. Battalions were usually sent back to Germany for new-equipment training on the *Panther*. Courses were held at the German base in Erlangen, near Nuremburg, which had a small training area, but any gunnery training had to be conducted at Grafenwöhr, which was the closest training area capable of conducting main-gun firing. The *G* version of the tank began to be issued in March 1944.

FACING PAGE TOP: A new *Panzer V, Ausführung D,* is prepared for rail movement. It is instantly recognizable as a *D* version by its drum-shaped commander's cupola. It may also be one of the last production batch of the *D*s before the *Ausführung A* was introduced, since it has a factory-mounted *Fliegerbeschußgerät* (antiaircraft ring mount). Note that it has left the factory with a base coat of *dunkelgelb* (dark yellow) and no other camouflage paint. Also of interest is the sign mounted on the railcar next to the tank: *Achtung! Ladung zu breit!* (Attention! Load too wide!). Trains carrying the *Panther* and *Tiger* family of armored fighting vehicles frequently had to be rerouted in Germany and other occupied European countries because they posed a safety hazard in certain tunnels and underpasses or on stretches of dual track, while passing other trains.

FACING PAGE BOTTOM: Brand-new medium half-tracks—the *Sd.Kfz. 251/1, Ausführung C*—leave the factory for army distribution centers. The *C* version of the half-track was produced from the beginning of 1941 until about August 1943, with half-tracks manufactured by the firm of Böhmische Leipa recognizable by their riveted construction. The light base color used on the vehicles may indicate that they were manufactured after early 1943, when the base coat of dunkelgelb was introduced.

ABOVE AND NEXT TWO SPREADS: This series of images shows the *Sturmgeschütz III* at the home front at various stages of the war. In the first image, an early assault gun is seen in a winter setting, probably during training. Due to the natural foliage used as camouflage and the posing of the crew, it cannot be determined which variant it is, although the short 75mm main gun indicates it is an earlier one. The *Ausführung E*, which was the last *Sturmgeschütz III* produced with the L/24 gun, was manufactured through February 1942.

ABOVE: This *Ausführung G* appears to have been photographed at a training detachment somewhere in Germany or northwestern Europe. The vehicle has been given a coat of whitewash, which must be considered somewhat unusual for a vehicle on the home front. One of the crew continues to wear the M34 overseas cap, while his comrade in the *Sturmartillerie* uniform wears the more current M43 billed field cap.

FACING PAGE TOP: In this image, the vehicle's black tactical numeral of *301* can clearly be seen next to the *Balkenkreuz*. A fresh coat of mud has been splattered over the running gear, which the crew will later have to try to clean off. The two visible crew members appear to be the same ones seen in the previous image.

FACING PAGE BOTTOM: The *301* moves down what appears to be a tank trail at a training area. It is followed at some distance by another assault gun. The whitewash appears to have been applied over a base coat of dark yellow, although the main gun barrel may have been replaced at some point, since it appears to have a darker-color primer coat.

FACING PAGE: These *Sturmgeschütz III, Ausführung G*s appear to be finished in dark gray, even though the M43 billed field cap that the officer is wearing in the first image suggests these photographs were taken in late 1943, at the earliest. This may be due to the fact that the vehicles are probably at a training detachment somewhere in Germany or northwest Europe. This particular battery has chosen to place its solid white tactical numerals behind the *Balkenkreuz* on the sideskirts.

ABOVE: An assault gun element is moved by rail, possibly to the front. A tarpaulin has been placed over the front portion of the fighting compartment to help prevent precipitation from entering.

ABOVE AND NEXT TWO PAGES: In this series of images, we see an armored scout company conduct railhead operations in preparation for a move, presumably to the front. The scouts belong to the heavy section of a company and are equipped with the *Sd.Kfz. 231 (8-Rad)*, which appear to be finished in a base coat of dark yellow. In the first image, the scouts all wear the same type of panzer tunic and trousers, but three different types of panzer headgear can be seen: the black version of the M34 overseas cap; the widely disliked black version of the M42 field cap (being worn by the scout on the viewer's extreme right); and the black version of the M43 billed field cap. The overseas cap predominates, since it was more popular for wear within the cramped confines of an armored fighting vehicle.

FACING PAGE TOP: An officer of the unit takes up a collection for an unnamed cause, but probably for the *Wintershilfswerk* (*WHW*), which all Germans, including the military, were "highly encouraged" to support during the war. The *Oberleutnant* is a combat veteran, as can be seen by his awards: the Iron Cross, First Class; a Black Wound Badge (for up to three wounds in combat); and an armored assault badge, possibly in bronze (for up to three separate armored engagements). He has also probably been in the *Panzertruppe* for some time, since he wears the first version of the panzer tunic, with the collar piped in branch color.

FACING PAGE BOTTOM: In contrast, the scouts appear to be conscripts for the most part, since few of them wear a combat decoration.

In the final two images, the scouts have donned the first-pattern reed-green herringbone-twill version of the panzer uniform to conduct the actual loading of their vehicles. It is interesting to note that the vehicles seem to have chock blocks applied to three sides of the wheels, as opposed to tracked vehicles, which normally only had the blocks applied to the front and rear of the tracks. The weaponry on the vehicles has been covered to protect it.

A factory-new *Panzer IV, Ausführung F2*, stands out in a field environment with its base coat of dark yellow. The tank is probably on the equivalent of a "shakedown" cruise by its crew or getting ready to conduct initial calibration firing. Of interest is the fact that many of the basic-issue items on the tank have also been painted in the basic primer color, including the spare track links on the right-hand fender. In contrast, the interior of the open hatches appears to be painted in red-oxide primer, even though exposed portions of the vehicle's interior were supposed to match the exterior color. The same is true of the Tetra fire extinguisher seen on the left fender. The crew members appear to be wearing the blue herringbone-twill panzer work uniform.

FACING PAGE TOP: An early *Panzer II* and *Panzer I* are seen in an open area, possibly at a training facility. As the war progressed, these vehicles were transferred to more mundane duties, especially for driver-training purposes. Neither vehicle has its weapons mounted.

FACING PAGE BOTTOM: In the second image, the crew of this *Panzerkampfwagen 35R (f)* talk to an officer, while some soldiers and noncommissioned officers conduct military sightseeing. Even obsolete vehicles such as these were impressed into service by the German Army, especially for use at training bases or for providing security in rear areas, thus freeing up more combat-worthy vehicles for the front. (MICHAEL H. PRUETT)

ABOVE: A Büssing-NAG 8.5-ton truck in the service of the *Deutsche Reichsbahn* (German Railways) displays some very interesting markings. The *Reichsbahn* emblem appears on the cab doors, and *Deutsche Reichsbahn* has been painted in large letters on the sides of the cargo bed. The truck is guarded by a noncommissioned officer, who has seen some combat, and two enlisted members, who appear to be recruits. Although the railroad would normally be responsible for guarding its own assets, the army might have become involved if sensitive items, such as weapons or optics, were being transported. This was especially true in occupied territories and even more so in the East, where the threat of partisans was ever-present. (MICHAEL H. PRUETT)

Training for scouts being assigned to the reconnaissance battalion of the *"Leibstandarte SS Adolf Hitler"* is conducted on the home front on the *Sd.Kfz. 231 (8-Rad).* The images were dated 1942, and the mountainous terrain in the background suggests the photos may have been taken at the Wildflecken Training Area, near the town of Fulda.

Scout vehicles were typically christened, usually with the name of a famous figure from German history or a German place name. In this case, however, the vehicle is named the "Eagle" (*Adler*).

Finishing out this chapter on supporting the war effort on the home front are 27 images taken from the album of someone closely associated with the development or procurement of the Trippel amphibian for the German armed forces and the *Waffen-SS*. Hans Trippel was a German automotive designer whose legacy is primarily the development of amphibious vehicles. Born in 1908, Trippel was a successful entrepreneur and started experimenting with the construction of amphibians in 1932 in Darmstadt. At the beginning of the war, he devoted himself exclusively to the construction of vehicles for the military. Because he was an officer of the *SS* and assigned to the *SS* Main Office, Trippel had the ear of high-ranking *SS* functionaries, including the *SS-Reichsführer* himself, Heinrich Himmler. This may partially explain the interest of the *Waffen-SS* in amphibious vehicles, although the *Volkswagen Schwimmwagen* seemed to be the main beneficiary of the *SS*'s interest, with production of Trippel's vehicles ceasing in 1944 in favor of the Volkswagen version, which was considerably cheaper and easier to manufacture.

In the first image, an *SG 6/41* (*Schwimmfähiger Geländewagen 6*, or "Amphibious All-Terrain Vehicle 6") is displayed at a factory showroom. A model of the vehicle is also mounted on a pedestal at the right front of the image. Introduced in 1941, some 800 to 1,000 of these vehicles in all their variants were apparently produced. (ALL IMAGES: MICHAEL H. PRUETT)

Apparently taken at a trade show before the war, high-ranking members of the *Marine-Sturm-Abteilung* (Naval *SA*) and the *Nationalsozialistisches Kraftfahrkorps* (*NSKK*; National Socialist Motor Corps) inspect a civilian Trippel amphibian on display. One of the dignitaries present is the commander of the *NSKK, NSKK-Korpsführer* Adolf Hühnlein. The vehicle features a polished black paint finish and non-military windshield.

Demonstrations of the *SG 6/41* are conducted for the *Luftwaffe*. Since the airmen seen in these two images are junior enlisted, the demonstration was probably an attempt to familiarize the personnel with the vehicle before they were used to assist in presentations for senior officials. The *SG 6/41* appears to be fully capable of propelling itself and towing two trailers across the calm waters of a small pond. The authors believe that these images represent the first photographic evidence of the use of Trippel's amphibious trailers.

The demonstrations continue, with three trailers attached. While the *SG 6/41* appears to be floating freely in the pond, the trailers seem to be riding along the bottom. The trailers are unique with their boat-shaped bow.

ABOVE: Here, army personnel are part of the demonstrations. At least 14 military personnel and the civilian driver can be seen, with the draft of the vehicle being essentially the same as when it did not have a complete load. The Trippel vehicles were bigger and more powerful than their *Volkswagen Schwimmwagen Typ 166* counterparts. Ultimately, the army preferred the Volkswagen and never adopted the Trippel *Schwimmwagen* for service.

FACING PAGE: Civilian personnel of the *Trippelwerke* and a military officer negotiate a steep incline with the *SG 6/41.*

ABOVE: The off-road capabilities of the *SG 6/41* are further demonstrated as it traverses a riverbank.

FACING PAGE: In this view, the convertible canvas roof is in place.

HERE AND NEXT TWO PAGES: In these images, two officers of the *SS* take a test drive in a small body of water with the *SG 6/41*. In the inserts, they are joined by additional employees of the firm, all of whom seem to be enjoying themselves. The officers, both *SS-Hauptsturmführer* (captain equivalent), are probably from the procurement office of *SS* headquarters, although both may have seen limited combat, based on their awards.

This combat engineer version of the *SG 6* bears *SS* license plates and is being inspected by officers of the *Luftwaffe*, with an officer of the *Sicherheitsdienst* (*SS* secret police) briefing them. The *Pionier* version had an enlarged body, which was capable of holding up to 16 combat engineers. In addition to the standard headlights, a Notek tactical night-driving light has been partially inset into the left front of the vehicle and an additional light seems to have been placed on right upper portion of the front hull. In the second image, an *SD* officer seems to be explaining some of the finer points of the vehicle to an attentive *Luftwaffe* general officer.

ABOVE AND FACING PAGE: Additional views of the *Pionier* version show the storage location for oars and docking aids.

A very rare photograph of the Trippel-designed prototype of an armed amphibious reconnaissance vehicle, the *Panzerspähwagen Schildkröte E3*, as it emerges from the company's testing pond. The "Turtle" was armed with a 2cm *MG151* in a fully rotating turret. By the time this prototype was developed in 1944, the army procurement office decided there was no longer a need for an amphibious armored car and cancelled the project.

Beginning in 1942, Trippel produced a version of the *SG 6/41 Schwimmwagen* with a coupe body style. These were intended to be used by the propaganda companies that accompanied the German armed forces in the field. The designation for the coupe body style was *SG-P*. This car has received a coat of whitewash with a large *Balkenkreuz* painted on the sides.

ABOVE AND FACING PAGE: The *SD* officer, an *SS-Sturmbannführer* (major equivalent), previously seen briefing the *Luftwaffe* party on the combat engineer version of the vehicle is seen here talking to two Trippel employees. The lead vehicle in the photographs is an *SG-P*, painted in a shiny black finish, while the standard *SG 6* brings up the rear and appears to have been finished in the dark gray of the time period. Like many of the Trippel vehicles seen throughout this series of images, the license plates on the vehicle are not standard *Wehrmacht* issue. Instead, they start with the letter *V*, which undoubtedly means *Versuchs* (test).

The final photograph from this album shows another invention of Hans Trippel, the *Kabinenschlitten*, a prop-driven "snowmobile" produced in 1943. Like almost all of his designs, it never left the prototype stage.

Notes

1 This position acted as an interface between the armed forces and the Nazi party.
2 Heinz Guderian, *Panzer Leader*, London, Arrow Books, 1990. p. 30.
3 The Czechoslovak tanks both weighed approximately the same, at 10.5 and 9.4 tons respectively, with armor of 25mm and armed with the *3.7cm KwK 34(t)* and 2 x *7.92mm MG37(t)*.
4 George F. Nafziger, *The German Order of Battle: Panzers and Artillery in World War II*, London, Greenhill Books, 1999.
5 The *Panzer I* was light at around 6 tons, had a crew of 2, was thinly armored at 13mm, and only armed with 2x*7.92mm MG13s*.
6 The *Panzer II, Ausführung C*, weighed 9 tons, had a crew of 3, hull armor of 14.5mm, and was armed with a *2cm KwK 30 L/55* automatic cannon and a *7.92mm MG34*. The main gun fired both high explosive and antitank ammunition and could penetrate 20mm of armor at 100 meters.
7 The first model of the *Panzer III* series to be produced in significant numbers was the *Ausführung E*. It was intended to be the main battle tank of the *Panzer* divisions. It weighed nearly 20 tons, had a crew of 5, maximum hull armor of 30mm, and was armed with a *3.7cm KwK L/46.5* and 2x*7.92mm MG34s*. Most tanks of this period, with a few exceptions, were armed with relatively small caliber main armament. Due to its limited production, some *Panzer* divisions in Poland did not have a single *Panzer III* in their inventory. The main armament was capable of penetrating some 64mm of 30-degree armor at 100 meters, this being sufficient to defeat most opposition tanks then in service.
8 The *Panzer IV, Ausführung C*, was designed as a medium support tank for the *Panzer III* and not intended to engage in tank-versus-tank combat. It weighed 19 tons—about the same as the *Panzer III*—had a crew of 5, hull armor of 30mm, and was armed with a *7.5cm KwK 37 L/24* and 2x*7.92mm MG34*. Although intended to primarily fire high explosive rounds, the armor penetration of the main gun was a quite reasonable 41mm of 30-degree armor. The *Panzer IV* was produced in small numbers in 1939 with some *Panzer* regiments only fielding 6 of these vehicles.
9 Thomas L. Jentz and Hilary Louis Doyle, *Panzer Tracts No. 23 Panzer Production from 1933 to 1945*, Maryland, Panzer Tracts, 2011. 34, 51.
10 Heinz Guderian, *Panzer Leader*. 73.
11 Research Institute for Military History, *Germany and the Second World War, Volume II, Germany's Initial Conquests in Europe*, Oxford, Oxford University Press, 1991. 263.
12 Nafziger, *The German Order of Battle*. 35.
13 Not all armored cars were combat vehicles. Many were signals vehicles within regimental and divisional headquarters. The Germans lumped all armored cars together when submitting readiness reports.

14 Nonetheless, both the British and French fielded the only marginally useful machine-gun tanks. In the case of the French, this was the Renault FT, dating from World War I. The British fielded the Vickers Mark VI, which was generally issued to cavalry units.

15 Jean Paul Pallud, *Blitzkrieg in the West Then and Now*, London, After the Battle, 1991. 64.

16 World War 2 Database: http://www.worldwar2database.com/gallery/wwii0053. The cited article presents additional information on this rare vehicle.

17 Peter Schmitz and Klaus-Jürgen Thies, *Die Truppen-Kennzeichen der Verbände und Einheiten der deutschen Wehrmacht und Waffen-SS im Zweiten Weltkrieg 1939–1945, Band 4*, Osnabrück, Biblio, 2000. 661-662.

18 The forces referred to as British included a sizeable number of Australian, Indian and South African troops.

19 Steven J. Zaloga, *Panzer IV vs Sherman, France 1944*, Osprey Publishing, Oxford, 2015.

20 Ludovic Fortin, *British Tanks in Normandy*, Histoire and Collections, Paris, 2005.

21 Walter J. Spielberger and Uwe Feist. *Panzerkampfwagen V Panther*, Feist Publications, 1968.

22 David Fletcher (editor), *Tiger! The Tiger Tank: A British View*, Her Majesty's Stationary Office, London, 1986.

23 *9. SS-Panzer-Division "Hohenstaufen"* and *10. SS-Panzer-Division "Frundsberg"* plus either the *12. SS-Panzer-Division "Hitlerjugend"* or the *21. Panzer-Division*.

24 An excellent adaption of the *Panzer IV* chassis, this tank hunter/assault gun had the same main armament and frontal armor as the *Panther*, although the 75mm L/70 gun was in a fixed superstructure with limited traverse. The weight of the vehicle was only 26 tons and about 140 were available for the Ardennes offensive.

25 Roddy MacDougall and Martin Block, *Panther, External Appearance and Design Changes*, Abteilung 502 Press, 2016. 278–79.

26 More than 4,000 wounded were flown out.

27 It is likely that this rebuilt division did not have its *Panzer* regiment. Instead, it only had a tank hunter battalion with two *Sturmgeschütz* batteries of 14 *StuG III*s or *IV*s each.

28 For those interested in these actions, see pages 93 through 112 of *Field Uniforms of Germany's Panzer Elite*. (Robert J. Edwards and Michael H. Pruett, Winnipeg, J. J. Fedorowicz Publishing, 1998.

Select Glossary

Abteilung (Abt.) Battalion equivalent (troop elements); detachment (training-base elements)
Ausführung (Ausf.) Model, variant
Flugabwehrkanone (FlaK) Antiaircraft gun
Kampfwagenkanone (KwK) Armored vehicle main gun
Motorisiert (mot) Motorized
Panzerabwehrkanone (PaK) Antitank gun
Panzerkampfwagen (Pz.Kpfw.) Armored fighting vehicle
Personenkraftwagen (Pkw.) Passenger car
Sonderkraftfahrzeug (Sd.Kfz.) Special-purpose vehicle
Sturmgeschütz (StuG) Assault gun
Sturmkanone (StuK) Assault cannon

Bibliography

Internet

Panzer World. "German Armor Camouflage." http://www.panzerworld.com/german-armor-camouflage. Good general introduction to German armor paint schemes and camouflage.

Tank Encyclopedia. http://www.tanks-encyclopedia.com. Good general information on all the vehicles discussed in this book.

Vehicles of the Wehrmacht. http://www.kfzderwehrmacht.de/Homepage_english/homepage_english.html. Very good information on wheeled vehicles and half-tracks in service with the Germany military.

World War II Multimedia Database. http://www.worldwar2database.com.

Books and Articles

Alman, Karl. *Panzer Vor*. Bochum, Germany: Heinrich Pöppinghaus Verlag, 1974.

Andorfer, Volker, Martin Block, and John Nelson. *"Marder III": Panzerjäger 38 (T) für 7,62 cm PaK 36 (Sd.Kfz. 139)*. Nuts & Bolts, vol. 15. Neumüster, Germany: Nuts & Bolts Press, 2001.

———.*"Marder III": Panzerjäger 38 (T) für 7,5 cm PaK 40/3 (Sd.Kfz. 138)*. Nuts & Bolts, vol. 18. Neumüster, Germany: Nuts & Bolts Press, 2004.

Bando, Mark. *Breakout at Normandy*. Osceola, WI: MBI Publishing Company, 1999.

Bender, Roger James, and Hugh Page Taylor. *Uniforms, Organization and History of the Waffen SS*, vol. 1. San Jose, CA: R. James Bender Publishing, 1969.

Bender, Roger James, and Warren W. Odegard. *Uniforms, Organization and History of the Panzertruppe*. San Jose, CA: R. James Bender Publishing, 1980.

Carius, Otto. *Tigers in the Mud*. Winnipeg, MB: J. J. Fedorowicz Publishing, 1992.

Chamberlain, Peter, and Hilary L. Doyle. *Encyclopedia of German Tanks of World War Two*. New York: Acro Publishing Company, 1978.

Cooper, Belton Y. *Death Traps*. Novato, CA: Presidio, 2000.

Davis, Brian L. *German Army Uniforms and Insignia, 1933–1945*. New York: Arco Publishing, 1983.

Dupuy, Trevor N. *Hitler's Last Gamble*. New York: HarperCollins, 1995.

Duske, Heiner F. *Panzerjäger I*. Nuts & Bolts, vol. 7. Uelzen, Germany: Nuts & Bolts Publishing, 1997.

Edwards, Robert J., and Michael H. Pruett. *Field Uniforms of Germany's Panzer Elite*. Winnipeg, MB: J. J. Fedorowicz Publishing, 1998.

Edwards, Robert J., Michael H. Pruett, and Michael Olive. *Scouts Out: A History of German Armored Reconnaissance Units in World War II*. Mechanicsburg, PA: Stackpole Books, 2013.

———. *Tip of the Spear. German Armored Reconnaissance in Action in World War II*. Mechanicsburg, PA: Stackpole Books, 2015.

Feist, Uwe, and Bruce Culver. *Panther*. Bellingham, WA: Ryton Publications, 1995.

————. *Tiger*. Bellingham, WA: Ryton Publications, 1992.

Feist, Uwe, and Wolfgang Fleischer. *Sturmgeschütz*. Bellingham, WA: Ryton Publications, 2000.

Feist, Uwe, and Thomas McGuirl. *Panzertruppe*. Bellingham, WA: Ryton Publications, 1996.

Fletcher, David, ed. *Tiger! The Tiger Tank: A British View*. London: Her Majesty's Stationery Office, 1986.

Fortin, Ludovic. *British Tanks in Normandy*. Paris: Histoire and Collections, 2005.

Gander, Terry, and Peter Chamberlain. *Weapons of the Third Reich*. Garden City, NY: Doubleday and Company, 1979.

Gill, Lonnie. *Tank Destroyer Forces, WWII*. Paducah, KY: Turner Publishers, 1992.

Greenland, Tony. "*Hummel*." Nuts & Bolts, vol. 10. Neumüster, Germany: Nuts & Bolts Publishing, 1998.

Greenland, Tony, and Detlev Terlisten. "*Nashorn*." Nuts & Bolts, vol. 14. Neumüster, Germany: Nuts & Bolts Publishing, 2001.

Guderian, Heinz. *Panzer Leader*. London: Arrow Books, 1990.

Harris, J. P., and F. N. Toase, eds. *Armoured Warfare*. London: B. T. Batsford, 1990.

Hettler, Dr. Nicolaus. *Schwerer Zugkraftwagen 12 TO and Variants (Daimler-Benz)*. Nuts & Bolts, vol. 16. Neumüster, Germany: Nuts & Bolts Publishing, 1999.

————. *Schwerer Zugkraftwagen 18 TO*. Nuts & Bolts, vol. 12. Neumüster, Germany: Nuts & Bolts Publishing, 1999.

Hoffschmidt, E. J., and W. H. Tantum IV. *Second World War German Combat Weapons*. Old Greenwich, CT: WE, 1968.

Jaugitz, Marcus. *Funklenkpanzer*. Winnipeg, MB: J. J. Fedorowicz Publishing, 2001.

Jentz, Thomas L. *Germany's Panther Tank*. Atglen, PA: Schiffer Publishing, 1995.

————. *Germany's Tiger Tanks*. Atglen, PA: Schiffer Publishing, 1997.

————. *Panzertruppen 2*. Atglen, PA: Schiffer Publishing, 1996.

Jentz, Thomas L., and Hilary Louis Doyle. *Panzer Production from 1933 to 1945*. Panzer Tracts, no. 23. Boyds, MD: Panzer Tracts, 2011. All books in the Panzer Tracts series (more than 20 and still counting) are recommended for those who want detailed, authoritative information on a particular vehicle.

————. *Panzerkampfwagen I. Kleintraktor to Ausf. B*. Panzer Tracts, no. 1-1. Boyds, MD: Panzer Tracts, 2002.

Kurowski, Franz. *Sturmgeschütze Vor!* Winnipeg, MB: J. J. Fedorowicz Publishing, 1999.

Kuusela, Kari. *Wehrmachtin panssarit Suomessa: Panzer Units in Finland 1941–1944*. Helsinki, Finland: Wiking-Divisioona Oy, 2000.

Lefévre, Eric. *La Wehrmacht*. Paris: Éditions Jacques Grancher, 1986.

————. *Panzers in Normandy: Then and Now*. London: After the Battle Magazine, 1983.

MacDougall, Roddy, and Martin Block. *Panther: External Appearance and Design Changes*. Abteilung 502, 2016.

McDonald, Jason. "Panzerkampfwagen B2 (F) Flammpanzer of Panzerabteilung (F) 102." World War II Multimedia Database, 2007. http://www.worldwar2database.com/gallery/wwii0053.

McKaughan, Jerry D. *Tech Intel*, vol. 1. Aberdeen, MD: Darlington Productions, Inc., 1994.

————. *Tech Intel*, vol. 2. Aberdeen, MD: Darlington Productions, Inc., 1995.

Münch, Karl-Heinz. *Combat History of Schwere Panzerjäger Abteilung 653*. Winnipeg, MB: J. J. Fedorowicz Publishing, 1997.

Nafziger, George F. *The German Order of Battle: Panzers and Artillery in World War II*. London: Greenhill Books, 1999.

Pallud, Jean Paul. *Battle of the Bulge: Then and Now*. London: After the Battle, 1984.

————. *Blitzkrieg in the West: Then and Now*. London: After the Battle, 1991.

————. *Rückmarsch! The German Retreat from Normandy: Then and Now*. Essex, UK: After the Battle, 2006.

Perrett, Bryan. *A History of Blitzkrieg*. London: Robert Hale, 1983.

Plowman, Jeffrey. *Orsogna: New Zealand's First Italian Battle*. Christchurch, NZ: Willsonscott Publishing International, 2010.

Plowman, Jeffrey, and Perry Rowe. *The Battles for Monte Cassino: Then and Now*. Essex, UK: Battle of Britain International, 2011

Pruett, Michael H. *Panzerkampfgruppe Strachwitz*. Winnipeg, MB: J. J. Fedorowicz Publishing, 2008.

Pruett, Michael H., and Robert J. Edwards. *Field Uniforms of German Army Panzer Forces in World War 2*. Winnipeg, MB: J. J. Fedorowicz Publishing, 1993.

Research Institute for Military History. *Germany and the Second World War. Vol. 2, Germany's Initial Conquests in Europe*. Oxford: Oxford University Press, 1991.

Restayn, Jean. *Tiger I on the Eastern Front*. Paris: Histoire & Collections, 1999.

———. *Tiger I on the Western Front*. Paris: Histoire & Collections, 2001.

Ritgen, Helmut. *The Western Front 1944: Memoirs of a Panzer Lehr Officer*. Winnipeg, MB: J. J. Fedorowicz Publishing, 1995.

Scheibert, Horst. *Panzer-Grenadier-Division Großdeutschland*. Warren, MI: Squadron/Signal Publications, 1977.

Schmitz, Peter, and Klaus-Jürgen Thies. *Die Truppen Kennzeichen der Verbände und Einheiten der deutschen Wehrmacht und Waffen-SS im Zweiten Weltkrieg, 1939–1945*. Vol. 1, *Das Heer*. Osnabrück, Germany: Biblio, 1987.

———. *Die Truppen Kennzeichen der Verbände und Einheiten der deutschen Wehrmacht und Waffen-SS im Zweiten Weltkrieg, 1939–1945*. Vol. 3, *Ergänzungen*. Osnabrück, Germany: Biblio, 1991.

———. *Die Truppen Kennzeichen der Verbände und Einheiten der deutschen Wehrmacht und Waffen-SS im Zweiten Weltkrieg, 1939–1945*. Vol. 4, *Kommandobehörden, Infanterie, Schnelle Truppen*. Osnabrück, Germany: Biblio, 2000.

Schneider, Wolfgang. *Tigers in Combat I*. Winnipeg, MB: J. J. Fedorowicz Publishing, 1994.

———. *Tigers in Combat II*. Winnipeg, MB: J. J. Fedorowicz Publishing, 1996.

Spaeter, Helmuth. *Die Einsätze der Panzergrenadier-Division Großdeutschland*. Friedberg, Germany: Podzun-Pallas-Verlag, 1986.

———. *The History of the Panzerkorps Großdeutschland*, vol. 2. Winnipeg, MB: J. J. Fedorowicz Publishing, 1995.

———. *The History of the Panzerkorps Großdeutschland*, vol. 3. Winnipeg, MB: J. J. Fedorowicz Publishing, 2000.

———. *Panzerkorps Großdeutschland, Bilddokumentation*. Friedberg, Germany: Podzun-Pallas-Verlag, 1984.

Spielberger, Walter J. *Beute-Kraftfahrzeuge und -Panzer der Deutschen Wehrmacht*. Stuttgart, Germany: Motorbuch Verlag, 1992.

———. *Die Halbkettenfahrzeuge Des Deutschen Heeres 1909–1945*. Stuttgart, Germany: Motorbuch Verlag, 1976.

Spielberger, Walter J., Hilary L. Doyle, and Thomas L. Jentz. *Leichte Jagdpanzer*. Stuttgart, Germany: Motorbuch Verlag, 1992.

———. *Schwere Jagdpanzer*. Stuttgart, Germany: Motorbuch Verlag, 1992.

Spielberger, Walter J., and Uwe Feist. *Panzerkampfwagen V Panther*. (Berkeley, CA): Feist Publications, 1968.

Takahasi, Yoshifumi. *The Last of the Kampfgruppen*, vol. 3. Tokyo: Dai Nippon Kaiga, 2001.

Zaloga, Steven J. *Downfall 1945: The Fall of Hitler's Third Reich*. Oxford: Osprey Publishing, 2016.

———. *Panzer IV vs Sherman: France 1944*. Oxford: Osprey Publishing, 2015.

Zetterling, Niklas. *Normandy 1944: German Military Organization, Combat Power and Organizational Effectiveness*. Winnipeg, MB: J. J. Fedorowicz Publishing, 2000.